Believing the Impossible before Breakfast

BELIEVING THE IMPOSSIBLE BEFORE BREAKFAST

ERNEST LEE STOFFEL

JOHN KNOX PRESS
ATLANTA

Library of Congress Cataloging in Publication Data

Stoffel, Ernest Lee.
    Believing the impossible before breakfast.

    Includes bibliographical references.
    1. Christian life—Presbyterian authors. I. Title.
BV4501.2.S77   248'.48'51   76–44977
ISBN 0–8042–2246–0

To Betty

"Wednesday Afternoon at 3:00"

The metabolism of the human body reaches its lowest ebb daily around three in the morning. The heartbeat slows, the blood pressure sinks to its lowest point during the twenty-four hours, and coronary care unit nurses watch their monitors more closely during the critical period, knowing a tired heart may choose that time to stop or start writhing in the frequently fatal complication of ventricular fibrillation. So it often is with the Christian spirit—except for a difference in time.

The low point in the strength of our faith is liable to come on Wednesday afternoon at 3:00 when—in the words of the author of this fine guide for Christians in believing some of the "impossible things" that form the basic tenets of our faith—"we are tired and have made fifty compromises that day already in our faith." A firm belief in the truth of such Christian "impossibles" as the resurrection of the body, a Son of God allowed by his Father to suffer a painful death as a sacrifice for the sins of ordinary people, the life everlasting, and dozens of other imponderables is never easy to maintain, even on Sunday mornings, with the organ and choir lifting our souls to a new concept of beauty in music and the preacher trying to expound the ancient truths of our creed in a way we moderns can accept—without too much painful searching of our souls.

By Wednesdays at 3:00, though, most of us are ready to throw in the towel for the rest of the week, hoping to get a new inspiration—a second wind for our faith—the following Sunday. What we need then, however, at a time when our spiritual metabolism is at its lowest ebb, is not a soothing voice, or even a reassuring platitude, but a man named Lee Stoffel quietly but firmly holding our noses to the grindstone, our feet to the fire, our shoulders to the wheel. A man who insists simply that we believe, in spite of all our doubts: "this insistence of the New Testament, this almost embarrassing insistence, flying in the face of everything, that God raised Jesus from the dead."

That's what this book is really all about and why it is so sorely needed by Christian and non-Christian alike. The author doesn't require that, like the Queen in *Through the Looking-Glass*, you believe as many as six impossible things before breakfast—or even the three big ones he challenges you with before the book is through. He settles for that one immutable truth and the way he explains it makes everything else, all the other impossibles, fall neatly into place, like the pieces of a jigsaw puzzle.

"How about wearing a sportcoat of faith instead of sackcloth and ashes?" he challenges the reader. Nor is it any happenstance that on a Sunday morning in Lee Stoffel's congregation, you'll find more men in bright sportcoats and women in colorful dresses—and no hats, praise God—than wearing the somber hues of traditional churchgoing. For the religion he teaches in this fine book, as well as from the pulpit with rare eloquence and conviction, is one of action, confidence, and happiness through the faith that, if God took the trouble almost two thousand years ago to let his Son die for us, he must think we're worth something after all.

God hasn't quit on you, the author of second Isaiah told the exiled Jews of Babylon, when their faith began to wane, and today Lee Stoffel is telling us the same thing when our spiritual metabolism is at a low point. Take this book with you every day —even to the golf course on Wednesday afternoons—and when you're in the rough or a trap, either literally or figuratively, stop and read a page or two. It may not increase your score in golf but it's bound to give you the courage to believe the impossible things your soul has been stumbling over. Moreover, you'll come out of the clubhouse wearing the sportcoat of faith for all to see, marvel at, and, maybe, imitate.

Frank G. Slaughter, M.D.
Jacksonville, Florida

Of Dr. Slaughter's fifty-five books published in twenty countries, twelve are novels with Biblical themes. The most widely read Biblical novelist of this or any century, he is a retired elder in the Riverside Presbyterian Church of Jacksonville.

A Word Before

In *Through the Looking-Glass*, the Queen said to Alice, who was standing in a world she couldn't believe: "I daresay you haven't had much practice. . . . Why, sometimes I've believed as many as six impossible things before breakfast."

The "world" of the Christian faith sometimes seems to be impossible to believe. Particularly "before breakfast"—when the bad dreams of the night are still with us and a demanding day before us. "Before breakfast"—when our own problems of living seem quite beyond any mention of God. "Before breakfast" time as far as faith is concerned can be anytime, as we know.

This book is written in the hope that you will travel with me into the world of the Bible and the Christian faith, hear its songs of joy, its trumpet-summons, its affirmations by which people have lived and died and grasped a victory.

It is designed to speak to us as we have to live in our times with some kind of commitment and a great deal of courage, while believing "impossible things," such as the resurrection and life after death, as well as believing that it is possible to live now with freedom and power. These "impossible" things may just turn out to be "possible"—for you. I hope so.

In any event, when the times are "out of joint," sometimes we are called to put them right. Sometimes we just have to live in them. Christians have elected not to curse their times, but to try to live with some kind of meaning and purpose—strengthened by faith. What is that faith? To this we turn.

Many people need to be thanked who have helped me. I am grateful to the people of four congregations: First Presbyterian Church in Maxton, North Carolina; First Presbyterian Church, Florence, Alabama; First Presbyterian Church, Charlotte, North Carolina (who encouraged me for seventeen years); and now the people of Riverside Presbyterian Church, Jacksonville, Florida. My wife, Betty, an author in her own right, has always given me the strongest kind of support. The book is dedicated to her. I express appreciation to my secretary, Holly Soud, who helped prepare the typescript.

It will be evident that I should claim no great originality and must freely acknowledge my debt to many teachers.

—Lee Stoffel

Riverside Presbyterian Church
Jacksonville, Florida

Contents

Living with God's Possibilities

What about living in today's world, considering this morning's headlines? Is it "possible"? These first three chapters talk about that from the standpoint of Biblical faith. You will be in the city of Jerusalem, for example, in the year 580 B.C. with a Babylonian army outside the walls. You will visit Jeremiah in the stocks. You will be with a poor widow scraping the bottom of a meal jar in a time of famine. You will experience the trauma of change which Israel faced when Moses died. But the emphasis is not on defeat. Quite the contrary. The difference is in believing God still has some possibilities he hasn't used yet.

1

It's Still Worth Living

In Shakespeare's *Hamlet,* Hamlet faces what seems to him the complete disintegration of his world. Everything at the court of his dead father, the former king, is now corrupt. His mother has connived at murder. His girl friend goes mad, and Hamlet, under the pressure of all this, cries out, "The time is out of joint. O cursed spite, That ever I was born to set it right." (I. v. 188) There have always been Hamlets in every age who have cried, "The time is out of joint." Cicero rose in the Roman senate to make his famous speech that began, "O tempora, O mores"— "O times! O morals!" And in the 1500s Montaigne, that famous French philosopher and very, very dark and pessimistic figure, wrote, "The age we live in is so dull and leaden that not only the execution, but the very imagination of virtue is hard to see." And in the 1600s John Tillotson, then Archbishop of Canterbury and the official historian of his time, wrote his whole era off by saying, "Men have hardened their faces in this degenerate age." And about the time that Columbus was on his way back from America, the *Nuremburg Chronicle* wrote: "The calamity of our time is such that iniquity and evil have increased to the highest pitch." And then the *Chronicle* gave its readers *six blank pages* to record the events from 1493 to the end of the world!

There have always been plenty who were ready to write off their times, and in our time there are plenty of prophets of doom who are ready to see this age written off, and who probably would not even give six blank pages to record events to the end of the world. And they have some cause.

The times are out of joint. They are out of joint on the national and international scene. Whether we like it or not, we are living in the middle of an age that the historians will surely call a time of world evolution—political and social; times that carry with them not only the flavor of evolution, but at times the very flavor of revolution. There are the social problems of the nation as we know, between the haves and the have nots. There is the decay of cities. There is a sense of moral exhaustion and a widespread belief that nothing works any more. And all of these unite to cause many people to throw in the towel. The times are out of joint. What can we say about living in a time out of joint?

First, and obviously, of course, we are surely held to our time. I say this is obvious, and yet it bears some saying again—particularly to those who want to escape somewhere else. We cannot escape forward or backward into time. We cannot move one inch from where we are now. If we could escape forward or backward, we would still have problems and pains, just different ones. Also, there is little use in covering our heads and crying doom and waiting for the end. The end of everything always comes sooner or later—but in its own time. And then there are those who enjoy the luxury of condemnation and denunciation; but that yields very little in the way of constructive help, it seems to me. For after the finger is pointed, what will the hand do to save? Denunciation is an illusory satisfaction and indeed, by itself, dangerous, as Jesus knew when he warned: " 'Judge not, that you be not judged.' " (Matthew 7:1) We are held to our times. We have to live in them and no other.

In the second place, one thing that the Bible tells us over

and over again is that we are called to live in our times and to be a saving people. Now this may sound like a crashing bore, but the Bible never seems to get tired of saying it. A time out of joint is always a time of opportunity as well as a time of upheaval and confusion. It can be a time of calling upon all that God has put within us—all that is just and worthy and honest and of good report—and I am not yet prepared to write us all off and to say that everything just and honest and worthy and everything of good report has gone by the board, because I don't think it has. We are called, perhaps not as spectacularly or as dramatically as Jeremiah or Martin Luther, but we are called to be a saving people just the same: to be sowers of good seed for future years for our children; to be a people of a joyous grace who judge not lest they be judged and who measure with the same measure by which they wish to be measured. If the posture of the Church is no more than condemnation without redemption, then we become like salt without savor, and our words will be cast out and trodden under foot. We are called to be a saving people—which is the positive, redemptive side of those who would do no more than condemn and denounce and deplore.

In 580 B.C. the Babylonians besieged the city of Jerusalem. They threw their siege machinery around it and after several months succeeded in piercing the wall. Their armies poured in and sacked and burned the city. And the prophet Ezekiel, who lived in that time, said, " 'I sought for a man . . . who should build up the wall and stand in the breach before me.' " (Ezekiel 22:30) For before the walls of that city were ever breached by the battering rams of Babylon, the walls of the home and the church and politics and society and government had already been breached, and God had been looking for men and women who would stand in the gaps and build up the wall before him. Long before any physical walls are breached, the spiritual walls have already been breached.

What does it mean to stand in the gaps and build up the wall? Well, for example, I think it means the strengthening of the home, where the covenant of marriage is respected. It means maintaining the integrity of government on every level —seeking to put what is right above what is expedient; where the employee is honest with the employer and gives an honest day's work; and where the employer respects the employee as a person with feelings and rights and needs. The gap in the wall is built up if in our present vexed time of public education we resolve not to abandon the public school system but to strengthen it on the principle that a wholly educated people is a free and productive people. I think it means Christian involvement in the power structures of the community and of the nation, for there are still such things as corrupt landlords and price gouging, and until someone stands in the gap in the power structure world, walls will be breached through which invaders will pour.

Jesus said to his disciples that they were to live as though they were stewards, stewards of everything, of all of life, given to them by the master of the house; and they were to take whatever had been given to them and were to conduct their affairs never knowing when the master of the house would return and demand an accounting. And he emphasized, " 'But of that day or that hour no one knows.' " (Mark 13:32) That is, it is futile and a waste of energy and time always to be thinking in terms of the end, and to be assured that the end is just around the corner and therefore there is nothing we can do or ought to do. "Of that day or that hour no one knows." And Jesus went on to say that the kingdom of God " 'is like a man going on a journey . . . [who] puts his servants in charge, each with his work.' " (Mark 13:34) We are stewards of all life under God the Lord of all life. In that sense we are called to be saving people —not pulling down people, not destructive people, but saving people—people who stand in the gaps and build up the walls. Without doubt this is going to require much study and thought and serious inquiry and new ways of thinking if we are going to be that kind of people in the present kind of world.

And in this study, of course, we must always look to ourselves. When put into the stocks, Jeremiah was fiercely disappointed and angry—he cursed the very day he was born; but at a certain point he left off lamenting and yielded himself to God —and that was all God needed. It will do no good to curse the times; instead, each of us must look to our own house, to our own soul, to our own sword and armor, to the state of our own relationship with God. As Gerard Manley Hopkins eloquently reminds us with these lines:

> *The times are nightfall, look, their light grows less;*
> *The times are winter, watch, a world undone:*
>
> *. . . . .*
>
> *Or what else? There is your world, within.*
> *There rid the dragons, root out there the sin.* [1]

" 'Watch therefore—for you do not know when the master of the house will come.' " (Mark 13:35) And the master of the house may come, not necessarily at the end of the world. The master of the house may come in that crisis which demands the resources of our souls. The master of the house may come at that time in the community when we clearly know what is right and what is wrong. The master of the house may come when suddenly a question is put to us and we have the opportunity of answering out of the strength and resources of our Christian conviction. That question may come at 10:30 on Wednesday morning.

What can we do when the times are out of joint? We can be a saving people; we can remember that we are held to our time and can escape to no other, and we can praise the Lord! Here is Jeremiah: "O LORD, thou hast deceived me." (Jeremiah 20:7) You told me to preach to these people and I did and I tried to tell them the truth and here I am in the stocks, and everybody's walking by spitting on me and cursing me and abusing me. "Cursed be the day on which I was born!" (Jeremiah 20:14) And I have great sympathy for the man—there in the public stocks, having preached to people, having said to them, "You know what you are doing is wrong. You know your society, your politics, and your government—and everything is shot through with corruption." And for his pains they put him in the stocks (a process by the way that I do not recommend for contemporary preachers); and they said, "All right, preacher, *now* what have you got to say?" And he said, "Cursed be the day on which I was born!" I have great sympathy for him. The man is in great anguish. But then at the end, there in the stocks before the temple with the spittle running down his face, he says, "Sing to the LORD, praise the LORD! For he has delivered the life of the needy from the hand of evildoers." (Jeremiah 20:13) That is faith, and that is where real theology gets itself done. Sing when you are held to the stocks and sing when you are standing in a time that is out of joint. Sing when the pressure seems to be so great that you can't stand it—sing, "Joyful, joyful, we adore Thee, God of glory, Lord of love." "To thee," says Jeremiah, "have I committed my cause." (Jeremiah 20:12) We can sing and we can still praise the Lord and believe he is the one who holds the outcome in his hands, saying, "thine is the kingdom and the power and the glory, for ever."

Some time ago, on a plane, I found myself sitting next to a gentleman and we exchanged names and what we were doing, and this time he didn't grow white when I told him I was a preacher! He said, "I am a Christian layman." And he said, talking to me as a preacher: "You know, we need help in our day; our country is in trouble, our children are in trouble, we are in trouble with our children, and we need someone to say to us, 'Keep on—it's worth it—it's worth it—keep on—don't hang up your guns, as it were, it's worth it—God has not left us.' "

While Cicero was crying doom in the Roman senate, Christ was about to be born in Bethlehem. Archbishop Tillotson cried "degenerate age," but this was also the time of a man named John Bunyan and the great Quaker George Fox. Montaigne saw no virtue at all in his time, but this was also the time of Martin Luther. And in 1493 when they gave us six more pages to the end of the world, a man named Columbus was coming back and saying there is a new world over there. "Cursed be the day"— curse the day if you will—who of us has not wanted to curse the day? Who doesn't want to do that now? Yet that won't light a single candle and it won't set right a single wrong. But say: "I will rejoice in the Lord"—say that, and regardless of the time, we shall be giving our hands and hearts to him who holds the wheeling stars in his hands—who holds us. And we shall be having our part with the wheeling of those stars.

*"As the LORD your God lives, I have
. . . only a handful of meal in a jar
and a little oil in a cruse.". . . "The jar
of meal shall not be spent and the
cruse of oil shall not fail."*
1 Kings 17:12, 14

2

Scraping the Bottom
of the Barrel

Suppose it all comes down to a handful of meal and a little
oil! John Buchan, the great mystery writer, says in the preface
to his masterpiece *The Thirty-Nine Steps* that he has an affec-
tion for "the romance where the incidents defy the probabili-
ties and march just inside the borders of the possible."[1] This is
where we are often called to live—just inside the borders of the
possible, with little more than "a handful of meal." A handful
of meal and a little oil by any standard is a starvation diet—mere
subsistence and little more.

This word comes alive for us at the point where our resources cannot be promised for tomorrow or even for this afternoon. "I have only a handful of meal." This comes out of a story
in the Old Testament of Elijah and the widow of Zarephath.
The heavens were dried up. A famine had come upon the land
and God told Elijah to go to a little village of Sidon and there
he would be fed. He comes upon a poor widow outside the gates
of the village late in the evening gathering sticks for the last
meal for herself and her son. He asks her for it and she gives it

to him in the faith that the jar of meal shall not be spent and the cruse of oil shall not fail.

Now this was a literal famine, of course, but there are other kinds of famine. There is the famine of affluence itself when we have got so much and a whole generation knows nothing else except now that it is beginning to run out and not satisfy. For things are not satisfying any more. There is the famine of youth flinging away from the culture and the things of their parents; and there is the famine of the parents who do not know what to do. There is the famine of power—enough in our day to destroy the world; and we continue to forge our swords into better swords into better swords into better swords. Power figures travel all over the world, and yet for all of the power and for all of the power figures we are not yet able to bring peace on earth and good will among us. There is even the famine of religion—religion that promises too much and cannot deliver and knows it and then goes after all kinds of tricks and gimmicks to get and hold the people. There is the famine of middle age when we have taken the measure of ourselves and the years come trailing after and the future is a blur. There is the famine of coming up against something that seems to tax our resources, and we know deep down inside ourselves that we cannot promise those resources for that thing—not this afternoon or perhaps even tomorrow. And like the widow of Zarephath we must confess, "I have only a handful of meal."

I think somewhere deep down inside all of us in this present age, we know this. Surrounded as we are by things—surrounded as we are with power such as Attila the Hun would have lusted after—having in our minds knowledge such as no other age has ever had. Yet deep down inside of us we know that these resources are not enough and so we turn to God. That is, we are told to turn to God. We are told that the place to turn is to God. And when we do *we learn that if God is to be trusted at all, he has to be trusted one day at a time.* The oil and meal —just enough for one day at a time. No more than that. Every time the widow of Zarephath went back to the jar of meal there was just enough there for that one day—and no more. I suppose we ought to pay credit to Elijah's faith here—he is the star in this story—but I really think that the credit goes to the faith of this poor widow. First of all, she had to give Elijah the very last meal for herself and her son and then she had to keep going back every morning and scraping the bottom of the barrel. Remember the widow in the New Testament story whom our Lord cited for her stewardship. She put in all that she had. But perhaps she ought to be cited more for her faith because no one ever thinks about the fact that she had to go home from the temple treasury and live after that.

Jesus taught us to pray, "Give us this day our daily bread." Apparently Jesus was quite serious about that prayer. He really meant that we should ask God for only one day at a time: "Give us this day our daily bread," and the original language literally reads: "Give us this day, each day, what we need a day at a time." He also said, " 'Do not be anxious about tomorrow' " (Matthew 6:34), for " 'your Father knows what you need.' " (Matthew 6:8)

A day at a time, without a full barrel in reserve. Now I don't know about you, but I want a full barrel in reserve! I feel much more comfortable if I know that I have got a full barrel and preferably two full barrels in reserve. One out in the garage as well as one in the pantry! How about you? We would rather have it this way and we would feel better about it when we pray: "Give us this day our daily bread."

Remember the parable of the rich fool who didn't rely on God every day but relied on his barns and every time he put up another barn he felt a little more secure and then finally he got to the point where he thought he really had it made—he had his security all arranged; no one could touch him; nothing could touch him—and then there came that dreadful voice in the middle of the night, " ' "Fool, this night your soul is required of you" ' " (Luke 12:20) And I have never thought it meant only that that man was going to die that night. It could mean that the man might have to go on living but there came into his life that night a demand for the resources of faith that he should have been storing up in his heart all these years. There came into his life a demand that cut across everything. "This night your *soul* is required." And he had not stored up those resources of faith. He put everything into the barns—he put everything into money, into things, into bank accounts—he put them into all of the material things that people think promise security. All through those years he had not stored up in his heart those resources of faith that would stand him in good stead when that "night" came.

Trusting God—one day at a time—is the only way I know that does it. If God only gives us one day at a time we can only trust in him one day at a time. We are strengthened in this by worship and prayer. In worship we sit down in the shadow of the cross of Jesus Christ and all that it means. We sit down in the shadow of the empty tomb. We have fellowship with the risen Christ. We pray: "God, here I am. You know me better than I know myself. I have all these things that concern me. I have the demands that shall be made upon me and I do not know what tomorrow's demands may bring. But God, you know me, and you love me and I count for something. And I am not alone. God, here I am."

And it is in that kind of faith and trust week after week, day after day, that we store up those resources of strength. It is in that kind of faith and trust that "things" take their place. The deal or the professional status that we long for or the social position or something else that yesterday looked so big and so important and so necessary—now begins to shrink and its voice begins to grow shrill. People take their place in this kind of faith: that person (perhaps of another color) who threatens me, or who I think threatens me; that person with whom I have great difficulty getting along; or that person I think does not like me. And all of us, rich or poor, troubled or happy, sinners who know it and sinners who don't know it—all of us become the children of God.

So we come finally to know in God's presence who we are; and to believe that in spite of what we are we are still loved. "Lord, I have only a handful of meal." And when I come to that point, then I must turn again to the one who leads me in the paths of righteousness, who restores my soul, who fills my cup and who prepares a table before me in the presence of my enemies—one day at a time.

"The jar of meal was not spent, neither did the cruse of oil fail." (1 Kings 17:16) That is, the resources of God are endless. Not that I expect my religion to be magic or that God will instantaneously and lavishly supply me with all my wildest dreams or even my best dreams. Not that I won't have any pain or illness or bereavement. Not that I won't have to keep going back to that jar of meal and see just enough for today and no more. But when I do go, I go to One whose resources are endless, whose providence is absolutely loving, whose promises will hold come hell or high water. "The steadfast love of the LORD," said the psalmist, "is from everlasting to everlasting." (Psalm 103:17) Measure the bottom of *that* barrel. "The LORD will keep your going out and your coming in from this time forth and for evermore." (Psalm 121:8) Measure that. Measure these words of our Lord: " 'your Father knows what you need.' " (Matthew 6:8) Or the words of Jesus to that poor woman at the well, torn by many a sin and racked by many a guilt, figuring that she was completely ostracized from God and humanity: " 'whoever drinks of the water that I shall give him will never thirst.' " (John 4:14) He is talking about the ever-flowing inexhaustible love and grace of a living God who loves us in spite of what we are and is ready to accept us and take us back again. Measure that jar of meal.

"I have only a handful of meal," but God has my hand. So everything runs out except God, and he is at the bottom of the barrel and he is in the famine and he is in the pain and he is in the hunger.

When God was trying to get Moses to go down to Egypt and deliver the children of Israel, it began to dawn on Moses just what that job really meant—that it really wasn't a simple thing at all. The promises that it carried with it were fine, but there was also quite a lot of danger. So Moses began to back away from the whole thing, as I think I would or you might. He makes all kinds of excuses and finally he says to God in effect, "Well now, what about you? Who are you? What is your name? Can I trust you if I am to take this job?" God told him his name, and it is translated, "I am that I am." It is a very difficult Hebrew word to translate. It might also be translated *"I will be there."* That says something to me. "Moses, go down to Egypt, confront Pharaoh, look him full in the face. You've got all kinds of things that are about to be thrown at you—all kinds of demands that are going to cut across your life and tax the resources of your spirit, but Moses, *I will be there!"*

Look at the bottom of your barrel. Look at that need. Look at that guilt. Look at that insecurity. "Moses, I will be there." " 'The jar of meal shall not be spent and the cruse of oil shall not fail.' " "Thou anointest my head with oil; my cup runneth over." (Psalm 23:5, KJV)

There is indeed a "miracle" here. The real miracle is in the freedom and in the power that comes from this kind of trust. Here is the miracle: "He gives power to the faint, and to him who has no might he increases strength." (Isaiah 40:29) Somewhere in my soul there is a little jar and there is only a handful of meal in it. There is never more than a handful in it but it is there and I keep going back to it. And my faith in God is there and my faith in prayer is there and my freedom and whatever power I have to make the day is there. Freedom is there, along with the power to make the day one day at a time; so I do not have to be bound by fear or guilt or insecurity. But I have to keep going back to it. Sometimes I see more of the empty jar than I do of the handful of meal on the bottom, and when I do I begin to lose some of my freedom and power. But then I reach in with the cup and I scrape the bottom, and there is still just enough of the love of God to make the day.

Now after the death of Moses . . . it came to pass that the LORD spoke to Joshua.

Joshua 1:1, KJV

3

Living with Change

Some "Moses" is always dying. Some Moses has died or will die for each of us. There is continuing change or a break in leadership. Sometimes it is a very traumatic kind of thing. The spotlight, for example, was thrown dramatically upon this for us a few years ago with the tragic assassination of President Kennedy. There was a break in leadership; an abrupt break, and the direction to which the nation had been looking had to be changed.

But this happens in lesser ways in almost every area of life. Moses dies. There is the collapse of old ideas and customs. Things are never as they were, though we keep trying to hold back the calendar or the clock. Old ideas die, old customs pass away. Youth's first ideas fail because they are immature, and even maturity knows its own disillusionments, discouragements, and disappointments. What we once thought was solid ground becomes shifting ground. We all know this experience.

Moses dies. There is personal disappointment and frustration. An ambition is smashed, or a person upon whom we had counted turns out to have feet of clay. Or something in our lives that we have counted on to carry us all the way suddenly is not there any more. And the strength and vigor of youth we thought would last forever doesn't. Moses dies.

But when Moses dies, God doesn't. "Now after the death of Moses . . . it came to pass that the LORD spoke to Joshua." This means at least that there is a continuity of something. Something goes on. There are some things that do not die. High in the Alps of Switzerland, you can climb a trial and believe that you have gone as far as you can go. At a certain point in the trial there is a sign that reads: "Das Ende der Welt"—"the end of the world." And you feel as though you have come to the end of the world. The clouds are far down below, and all the towns down below look very small. But all you have to do is push ahead, just a little farther around the hill and the trail goes on. The sign wasn't true. This is what the first chapter of Joshua says. "Now after the death of Moses"—everyone was wailing and weeping and saying "Das Ende der Welt." This is the end of the world. We go no farther. Everything is gone and everything is lost. But then, "the LORD spoke to Joshua."

When Moses dies, does God? Well perhaps that can be answered easily in just one word, "No." It can be answered in one word, but not easily. When Moses dies, does God? We can say no to that. But you don't say that easily. You just don't let that roll off your tongue without some deep, solid thinking. For one thing, it means a tremendous no to all our fears and our anxieties: the time when the thing upon which we have counted dies and it seems as though God has died.

It means also that God does not stand helpless when truth and right seem to be defeated. I have seen people literally tear up everything and fling it in God's face when their own particular little program (and it may have been quite a good one) seemed to fail for the moment. I have seen people tear up everything and fling it in God's face when it seemed that truth and right were defeated. And they said, God is dead.

It means that God does not stand helpless before our disappointments and frustrations or our besetting sin, or before that fear which strikes like a cold chill when some Moses dies, and we stand before Jordan. We have heard it said: "She believed in God until her husband died." Or, "he believed in God until Freud" or the theory of evolution or something else. It means that just because our ideas about God and faith in the Church and the gospel have failed, or have to be changed (and they do), God hasn't died. It means that just because youth has passed and old age has come upon us, God hasn't died. It means that just because that Moses whom we have followed and have depended upon for so long has suddenly fallen before us, God hasn't died.

And this is why I say we cannot easily answer this question in one word. We do think God is dead. It is not an easy thing to say no to. We have to stand before this thing, whatever it is, before we answer too glibly. At the same time, if we are prostrate when some Moses dies, then it may be that Moses is our God.

When Moses dies, God doesn't and moreover, Jordan is not the limit. Again, in the first chapter of Joshua, we see Joshua and the children of Israel on the banks of the Jordan. Moses is dead. Perhaps the promise to Abraham is dead also. Perhaps God cannot deliver. It is all over. Perhaps everything did die with Moses. Then there comes this word of the Lord to Joshua. " 'Every place that the sole of your foot will tread upon, I have given to you. . . . From the wilderness . . . to the Great Sea toward the going down of the sun.' " (Joshua 1:3, 4)

Jordan is not the limit. This is to say, God's promise always exceeds anything that we can ask or think. Here is the promise in Isaiah, for example, in a classic passage: " 'though your sins are like scarlet, they shall be as white as snow.' " (Isaiah 1:18) Or the promise in John: "Beloved, we are God's children now; it does not yet appear what we shall be." (1 John 3:2) And, once, Jesus of Nazareth came upon a group of men at their trade of fishing. Their world was mainly concerned with those boats and nets and the Sea of Galilee, and no more. But one day, Jesus of Nazareth said to those men: " 'Follow me, and I will make you fishers of men.' " (Matthew 4:19) And a whole world opened up. Their world became no longer the fishing boats and the nets. Andrew and Peter and James and John became the fishers of men. Jordan is not the limit. Paul said it another way: "Now to him who by the power at work within us is able to do far more abundantly than all that we ask or think, to him be glory." (Ephesians 3:20) And isn't this the deep meaning of the resurrection of Jesus Christ? It is trying to say to us: "No Jordan. This earth is not the limit."

Some will say, "I don't believe that. It sounds good in church, but I don't believe that. I don't believe God can do anything with me or for me. Moses is dead, and that's the end of it." Joshua and Israel would never have found out if they hadn't crossed the Jordan. They could have said: "It very well may be that though Moses is dead, God isn't. And perhaps God will be with us and will do great things for us. But we are afraid to try. We will stay safely here on this side of the Jordan." But Joshua said to the officers of the people, " ' "within three days you are to pass over this Jordan, to go in to take possession." ' " (Joshua 1:11)

The only way they could find out whether or not God meant it or whether God could do it was to cross the Jordan. With courage. It takes courage to walk with God in this life and to believe that when Moses dies God doesn't. Three times God said to Joshua, "Be strong and of good courage." God knows that sometimes it takes everything within us to walk the life of faith. And it takes obedience. Here is this word of the Lord to Joshua: " 'This book of the law shall not depart out of your mouth, but you shall . . . be careful to do according to all that is written in it.' " (Joshua 1:8) So there is no cheap grace, no cheap possession of God's land. That vigorous soul-searching word is there: " 'turn not.' " (Joshua 1:7)

It took obedience and faith. By that, I mean it took the kind of faith to believe that the Lord was with him. At least twice God said to Joshua, "The Lord your God is with you." But it takes faith to believe that God is with us—he does not knock on our door and say, "Now get up, my friend. I am going to be with you today in everything you have to face. Here is a shining glorious angel just above your head!" God doesn't work that way. He tells us that we have to get up every morning and put our clothes on and eat breakfast and go out into the world with the faith that he is with us. And when Israel stands still, when people stand still before these promises of God, particularly as they are given to us in his son Jesus Christ, then they never inherit the promised land.

It may be that we have never committed ourselves to faith and Christ. Some of us may need to make an honest repentance. Others of us may have to admit some disappointment or loss. Perhaps we never have. Perhaps we have put it behind us and kept saying, "I will look at that the day after tomorrow," but perhaps we need to face that disappointment or that loss and put aside the bitterness and go with God across the Jordan. Moses may be dead, but God isn't. His possibilities are endless. What can God do with us and for us? We will never know until we commit ourselves. We will never know, unless by faith, we go over into God's land whose boundaries are beyond the going down of the sun.

Living with God's Salvation

Now we need to talk about something called "salvation." Sometimes we see the word *saved* on a road sign while trying to make a sharp turn. Or a preacher will mention it. Sometimes it will cross our minds: What does it mean to be "saved"—if anything? Is it possible to believe in salvation—God's salvation that is—and what does it mean if we do believe? The next two chapters are written close to the Lord's Supper, the Eucharist, "communion." What on earth is salvation? Where is the real power in believing in God's salvation? We will talk about believing in the real center of Christian faith, the resurrection. *That* faith is trying to do something for us as Christians and also as the Church. In short, it is trying to pick us all up off the floor!

4

What on Earth Is Salvation?

"Salvation" is one of those words so often used in church that it has become faded and has lost much of its original thrust and power. We think of "going to heaven" or having our sins forgiven or perhaps both. But I expect if we are honest there isn't much excitement about it, to say nothing of passion. No excitement, for example, as there was in Paul when he said: "To me, though I am the very least of all the saints, this grace was given, to preach . . . the unsearchable riches of Christ." (Ephesians 3:8) When we come into a church and see the Lord's Table—a symbol of the salvation that God has done for us in Christ—I doubt that we say "to me, though I am the very least . . . this grace was given." Can we identify with the anguished cry that was wrenched from Paul in the seventh chapter of Romans: "Wretched man that I am! Who will deliver me from this body of death? Thanks be to God through Jesus Christ"? How many times have we said that when we think about the salvation which God has done for us? And even we preachers often use the word "salvation" without excitement.

In the Lord's Supper, the Eucharist, we get very close to this "salvation": "This is my body broken for you. This is my blood shed for you." Here we look at and we are told about the sacrifice that God made for us in Christ. We look at the signs of sacrifice and pain beyond human imagining and we eat and drink the symbols of that sacrifice.

In this Jesus is a saving presence. No matter how vague our faith may have become, no matter how many things press in upon us that tend to separate us from the things of our faith and religion, at the Lord's Table we can all say that in some way we find it true that here we are struck again with the vivid memory of Jesus Christ, and of what he did for us, and it carries with it a "salvation."

Now Christians have always believed that. Our Roman Catholic brothers and sisters believe that the bread and wine actually become Christ's body and blood. Our Lutheran brothers and sisters believe that he is "around" the bread and wine in some way. Presbyterians and others believe that he is spiritually present, even though the bread remains bread and the wine remains wine. And perhaps we are all partially right, and none of us is really absolutely correct. Perhaps all of us are groping for something that we feel more than we can express: that Jesus Christ is more present here—that he becomes here our salvation—that in that presence, in his broken body and shed blood and in the signs of that body and blood which we eat and drink, he does something for us that we could not do for ourselves. And if all the theologians of all the ages were brought together in assembly, I doubt if any of them could ever come out with a precise, written definition of this, but I think all of them and all of us together could say we feel this "presence" and this "salvation."

God's salvation comes home to us in the Supper in a very special way. We know and we feel deeper things than words can say. Forgiveness becomes more than just a casual word. We hold out our hands to God and receive his salvation. And we know what Peter was trying to say when he wrote to the first-century Christians, "You know that you were ransomed . . . not with perishable things such as silver or gold, but with the precious blood of Christ . . . without blemish or spot." (1 Peter 1:18-19)

But it would not do to stop and be satisfied with just saying this. There is something else about this salvation: *it expects something of us.* And this, I think, is where it becomes real. God says to Israel on the other side of the Red Sea: " 'You have seen what I did to the Egyptians.' " (Exodus 19:4) The Lord is saying to the children of Israel: "Look at my salvation—you've seen what I did." But he does not stop there: " 'Now therefore, if you will obey my voice and keep my covenant . . . you shall be to me a kingdom of priests.' " (Exodus 19:5,6) There is an expectation laid upon them. God's salvation always expects something of us. Think about this for a moment: unless that sense of expectation is there, we feel cheated, and we believe that something is wrong. We can't quite define it, but we know that something is wrong. We feel that forgiveness cannot be that cheap, and it isn't.

While driving on a busy highway, I happened to find myself approaching a traveling van. As I got closer I saw a sign on the back of it that read: "Being Saved Can Be Fun!" Now it so happened that the apostle Paul was riding with me, and he also saw that sign—not literally, you understand, I haven't taken leave of my senses—but I could almost hear Paul stir uneasily on the seat beside me and say, "Can stoning and lashes and fighting the lions in the arena be fun? Can giving up all for Jesus Christ be fun?" Now of course, there is a very, very small sense in which that word is true—to know Jesus Christ and to know his salvation is to know a freedom and a realization and a joy and an inner peace that I suppose you could call "fun." But the New Testament speaks of an expectation that is laid upon those who receive this salvation, and I think the New Testament would say we must think in bigger dimensions than "fun."

God's salvation expects something of us. I hear Jesus talking about denying ourselves and taking up the cross. When God's expectations begin to move in on us as we think about our daily lives, asking hard questions about ourselves, our behavior, our decisions, our human relationships, our family relationships, our church relationships, the quality of our lives and of our commitments—*then* God's salvation begins to become a serious thing. There is nothing casual or cheap about it. There is nothing casual or cheap about the cross. Indeed about this whole matter of salvation, God is as serious as hell!

If we have lost the feeling of expectation and feel no demands, no questioning of ourselves, no sense of commitment, then it is time to ask why—which is where the Lord's Supper picks up meaning and becomes more than a ritual. So we hear the old words said: "This is my body broken for you. This is my blood of the new covenant which is shed for many for the remission of sins." And we take in our hands the tangible signs of God's salvation—the bread and the cup—where we believe that the Savior is especially present in saving power. Private things should pass between us and the Lord. Paul says, "Let a man examine himself and so eat . . . and drink." (1 Corinthians 11:28) A transaction should take place. We will ask for forgiveness. If questions are asked of us and we hear some claim or expectation, be glad—for this is where God's salvation begins to happen.

And when he had given thanks, he
broke it, and said, "This is my body
which is for *you."*
1 Corinthians 11:24, emphasis added

5

Believing Someone Is for Us

Albert Camus writes somewhere about the "walls against which we go agroping, the places still invisible, where gates may open."[1] "The places still invisible where gates may open." So we grope along walls—looking for deliverance and freedom —a place where the gate opens.

How can we be delivered from sin, which binds the human spirit, builds walls around us and separates us from other people, saps energies, clouds conscience? Can we be delivered from death itself—the bringer of tears and separation, that most dreaded and final wall of separation? Is there a "gate" in the wall?

As Christians, we are like Moses and the children of Israel standing on the other side of the Red Sea, singing " 'The LORD ... *has become* my salvation.' " (Exodus 15:2, italics added) For we think of the death and resurrection of our Lord, Jesus Christ, as God's great "deed." And the "deed" at the Red Sea is but a small suggestion of that deed which God did in Jesus Christ, "for us men and for our salvation." "For by his death, he destroyed the power of death"—so goes an old affirmation of Christian faith—"and by his glorious resurrection, he has opened the kingdom of heaven to every believer." It is as though a great gate has been swung open that no one can shut; and no devil in hell and no angel in heaven can bar. A great door is opened by the love of God and on the other side of that door is freedom and deliverance.

Where does this gate open for me? How do we know? How can we enter this gate? It is at the point where we believe that God really is *for* us, and not against us. "This is my body which is *for* you." Hear this as something being said to *you* for the first time, perhaps. "This is my body which is for you. This is my acceptance which is for you. And if you will, this is my humanity and your humanity gathered up in the flesh of the Son of God which is for you."

This is where the gate opens: where we decide in mingled repentance and joy and tears and laughter and all of the emotions that are somewhere deep down inside our hearts that we cannot let get out and dare not—where we decide, there in that mingled pool, that God really is *for* us. Even in the face of our own contradictions. And God knows and we know what a mass of contradictions we bring to him. Even in the face of that, he is *for* us. As Jesus was for the thief on the cross, he is *for* us. There was that poor soul shouting across to Jesus on the other side of him, " 'Jesus, remember me when you come in your kingly power.' " (Luke 23:42) The thief saw something in that man who was being crucified with him. Just ahead of him a gate was opening and he wanted to go through that gate. And there is Jesus shouting back across the gulf, " 'today you will be with me in Paradise.' " (Luke 23:43) You will go through that gate! And the man grasped that promise and went through. So Jesus is shouting to us across whatever gulf. There are so many "gulfs": indecision, guilt, rejection, doubt, depression, selfishness, loneliness. Those are just a few. Jesus is shouting to us across the gulf, "This is my body which is for you."

He opens something for us at that point when we decide that he is for us. He opens for us a spiritual relationship with God. The mystery that surrounds us—the unanswered questions that always surround us—that mystery becomes love. And that love takes our repentance and puts forgiveness around it; takes our pain and puts hope around it. "This is my body which is for you." This is a gate opened not to escape but to a new life and to new hope where sin and death and that present pain, whatever it is, do not have the final word.

The "walls against which we go agroping, the places still invisible, where gates may open." We are all feeling along that wall—with hopes and fears and guilts that nag, perhaps lonely inside, perhaps blocked off from realizing our full potential by a thousand pressures that are like gateless walls. We grope along for the opening. Here is the opening: "This is *for you*." We don't have to grab at it; or worry about being worthy of it. God is for us, as when we say to a friend in trouble, "I am for you." This is salvation.

And Peter opened his mouth and said: "Truly I perceive that God shows no partiality, but in every nation any one who fears him and does what is right is acceptable to him."
Acts 10:34–35

6

Believing Someone Is for the People

Suppose there were something in this world that refused to allow any walls to be built around it? There is. It calls itself the Church of Jesus Christ—a community of faith that God is for us, and that he has shown he is for us in Jesus Christ. Those who believe God is for them form a community of faith called the Church. At least, this is what happened to the first disciples of Jesus, after Good Friday and Easter. A community of faith happened—which discovered that it has no walls; that it holds something within it that tears down every wall erected around it. But it had to be worked out. And it has to keep on being worked out. This is the way it went in the beginning . . .

After Easter, after Pentecost, the Church was thrust out upon the streets of the world to preach the gospel of Jesus Christ. Almost immediately a question arose: What about the Gentiles? The first Christians were Jews. Was Christianity to remain a sect within Judaism—that is, must a convert become a Jew before becoming a full-fledged Christian? Would the Christian Church open freely to the world? The issue was soon put before the Church. And it began with a remarkable meeting between the apostle Peter and a Roman centurion named Cornelius.

Two worlds met in the house of Cornelius that day. On the one hand, the world of Peter: the Palestinian Jew, descended from Abraham; a man who had, from his youth, been taught to respect with his very life the laws of Moses and the traditions and rituals of the Jews. And on the other, the world of Cornelius: the Roman, representing the masters of the world, representing the occupation forces of Peter's country. And not only that, he was a Gentile; therefore, one whose house Peter, as a Jew, was not permitted to enter; and if he knew it, he would not even sit in a chair that had been occupied by a Gentile! Imagine the struggle that took place within Peter. It had already begun in his experience on the housetop at Joppa, when he saw a sheet let down from heaven with all kinds of clean and unclean animals in it and a voice said, " 'Rise, Peter; kill and eat.' " (Acts 10:13) And immediately conflict came to Peter, a Jew. Could he eat animals that his Mosaic Law called unclean? And yet he heard, " 'Rise, Peter; kill and eat. . . . What God has cleansed, you must not call common.' " (Acts 10:13, 15) After this experience, which grew out of Peter's faith in the whole gospel of Jesus Christ, Peter went to Cornelius; he entered his house; he sat down at his table; and Peter opened his mouth (and this time, bless his heart, he didn't put his foot in it). Peter opened his mouth and said, " 'Truly I perceive that God shows no partiality.' " He preached the gospel to Cornelius and to his household; he baptized them and received them into the fellowship of the Church. And the walls came tumbling down. At that moment walls began to come down between Jew and Gentile, male and female, slave and free, Greek and barbarian; in a world where Jews spat on Gentiles and Gentiles spat on Jews; where the status of women was ranked with that of children and slaves. The walls began to come down; and they have been coming down ever since. There are some affirmations in this whole scene that came to a focus in the words of Peter: " 'God shows no partiality.' " (Acts 10:34)

Obviously, one affirmation is that the Christian Church can

never build walls about itself. God's purpose, from Abraham on, did not intend that it should all end with Peter turning away from the door of Cornelius; that it should all end in an obscure Jewish sect (as it could very well have done, because there were many sects within Judaism). God did not call Abraham and through him a people, and then weary and suffer with those people through many generations, and then finally send his Son, so that it would all end with Peter turning away from the door of Cornelius. The very nature of the gospel refuses to know a wall. It leaps over boundaries, it tears down walls. Christianity is never a movement within any cultural or social group. Christianity and the Christian gospel can never be a prisoner, for example, of Episcopalian liturgy or Baptist baptism or Presbyterian creed. Christ, said Paul, "has broken down the dividing wall of hostility." (Ephesians 2:14) And the Christian faith does not belong to either East or West, North or South, but it affirms in the words of Paul: "There is neither Jew nor Greek, . . . neither slave nor free . . . neither male nor female; for you are all one in Christ Jesus." (Galatians 3:28)

No walls there! No way to build a wall. This went hard for many in the Church at Jerusalem. It always does go hard. There is a sense in which this has to be discovered in every generation. When Peter returned from the house of Cornelius and reported to the church in Jerusalem, he was not met with rejoicing, he was met with rebuke. Instead of rejoicing that a door had been opened by the grace of God into the whole world, they said to Peter: "Why have you, a Jew, entered the house of a Gentile?" And not only that, but Peter had dared to receive him into the fellowship of the Christian Church. The remarkable thing is that Peter, a provincial Jew, refused to ally himself with that group within the Christian Church that would have from the very beginning built the highest possible wall. In essence what they wanted was a requirement that anyone hoping to become a member of the Christian Church must first become a Jew. Every new member must be—"like us."

And Peter refused to ally himself with that. Why? Because the gospel refused to let him do it. He remembered Jesus and the Samaritan woman—the day that Jesus sat down by the well and talked to her—first of all a woman and second a Samaritan. He remembered that Jesus went to lunch with Zacchaeus, that traitor to his country. He remembered Jesus going in—despite the murmurs of the self-righteous crowd—to eat with publicans and sinners. And he remembered that day when Jesus cast his eyes around the crowd in which there were no doubt many Gentiles and said: " 'many will come from east and west and sit at table with Abraham, Isaac, and Jacob in the kingdom of heaven.' " (Matthew 8:11) But I think that above all Peter remembered the cross. He began to grasp what that cross really meant for him and for the whole world. Later at that all-important Jerusalem Council (which was the first of many councils), when they had to fight this thing out, there was the Judaizer party and there was the party of Paul and Peter. The great debate took place—within that council the issue was to be decided whether the doors would be shut; whether Christianity would become a mere obscure dying sect within Judaism. Peter got to his feet and found his tongue again and said to the assembly of the Church: we believe the Gentiles will be saved through the grace of Jesus just as we will (Acts 15:11). The Church's gospel will not let her build walls.

"God shows no partiality." The gospel is a gospel *for* the world. Cornelius is the man without Christ, yes. Cornelius is the man who knows nothing of the love of God, suffering from the desolations of sin and death, yes. And we must never lose sight of that. Christianity is a personal God for the person within the depths of his or her own being. It is a renewing force; it is a forgiving force, it has a word to say to the desolations of the inner person. But it has more than that to say. Cornelius may also be, for example, the world of science, of labor, of business, those places where people are involved in the great operations of the world, transporting, designing, selling. The gospel is not only for the desolations of sin and death, but also for the world because the gospel says that God is *for* the world. This affirms the worth of persons, the importance of the earth and its resources; the right of people to live in freedom, dignity, and peace. Do we not believe that God created it all? So we affirm the rights and freedoms of human beings. God must be concerned not only about saving my soul from death and hell, but, also, this world in which I live.

And the Church has to go to Cornelius with this gospel, humbly and without moralizing, both telling and showing that we do believe in the love of God for all people. Perhaps a powerful clue for us is this: Cornelius saw Peter come into his house, sit down with him at his table, break bread with him, and above all else, deal with him as a human being. And thus, Peter preached before he ever opened his mouth. I suppose we ought to admit that we haven't found out how to go to Cornelius today. This is part of the evangelistic dilemma of the Church; partly because the gospel is still battering down the walls around the Church and partly because we honestly do not know yet. But we haven't given up. We are still trying.

There is a third affirmation here in this scene in the house of Cornelius, and in this truth which Peter put into words: "God shows no partiality." Not only can the Church not build walls about itself, not only is the gospel we have a gospel for the world; but there is this: *Christ is there with Cornelius waiting for us.* That is what Peter discovered when he entered the house, rather uncertain, with all kinds of conflicts churning around inside of him, unsure of his ground, but feeling he must go in obedience to the redeeming gospel of Christ. He found his Lord already waiting there for him, in a place he never expected to find him; in a Roman Gentile household! And I suppose that that was as unthinkable for him as it is for us to think of finding Christ in a labor union meeting or a board of directors meeting, or maybe with that person we do not like, or that person of another race who may appear threatening to us, or that person putting up a hostile air. But then Jesus did say, didn't he, that we would find him with the sick, the hungry, the stranger, the imprisoned, the naked. He said that at the last judgment there would be many people surprised: " 'I was hungry and you gave me food, I was thirsty and you gave me drink, I was a stranger and you welcomed me. . . . as you did it to one of the least of these my brethren, you did it to me.' " (Matthew 25:35,40) Can we find it within ourselves to take this gospel and to go to Cornelius, wherever Cornelius may be, and show and tell him that the love of God is for him and his world, that he need no longer be a stranger? There is where we find Jesus Christ.

And walls begin to come down. They keep coming down before this gospel. What a treasure this gospel is; what a treasure Peter took with him that day into the house of Cornelius. It is the word of hope which says to everyone: You need not be a stranger or an enemy. God is for you; God is for the world, for all good hopes, for all the good and gracious things which make for peace and wholeness and health upon this earth. Christ is our peace who has broken down and keeps on breaking down the dividing walls of hostility. Would you believe no walls?

"this Jesus . . . God raised him up."
Acts 2:23, 24

7

Where Is the Power?

"Church Growth Sags to New Low!" Every so often one sees such a headline. Some are saying that the Church lacks power today. By that I think they mean that we in the Church have become a pretty tame lot—not really bothering anyone—not really having much influence in the mainstream of things. That may be. Of course, we shouldn't measure power in the same way that the world measures power—that is, in the ability to push people around and command events. But when it comes to the power of inner conviction that is something else. And sometimes when I measure myself against those first Christians who endured dungeon, fire, and sword, I wonder. I suppose we all do. When I look at churches becoming clubs catering to the comfortable pew, I wonder. When I see tendencies of that in myself and in the churches, I wonder.

Well, the power is where it has always been. *The power is in the faith that God raised Jesus from the dead.* The first Christian sermon, the first time a Christian preacher, the apostle Peter, opened his mouth, he said, " 'this Jesus . . . God raised him up.'" (Acts 2:23, 24) He didn't say "My friends, we have a great ethic for you—we have a great program for a magnificent church, we have splendid plans for organizations and committees." He said, "this Jesus . . . God raised him up" as if that were enough. And, later on, he wrote to some fellow Christians: "you have confidence in God, who raised him from the dead." (1 Peter 1:21)

Now, somehow, we have to work our way back to that, and it isn't easy. It fits on Easter and at funerals—at funerals because we want desperately to hear it and we need to hear it; at Easter because it is the prevailing mood. But what about Wednesday afternoon at 3:00? When we are tired and have made fifty compromises that day already in our faith? But suppose the New Testament could get a chance with us and we really believed this insistence of the New Testament, this almost embarrassing insistence, flying in the face of everything, that God raised Jesus from the dead?

At least when we get there we are at the heart of the matter. Even if we can't understand it fully, we understand somehow that when we get there the issue is really joined, that we are "where it's really at," as far as the New Testament is concerned. We are no longer in the shallows—content to dabble in pious emptiness, shaking a vague finger somewhere in the direction of morality, wherever morality went; or else found frantically trying to search out what people want and give it to them in hopes that rolls may swell and attendance increase. And if all else fails, we can always use the Church to shore up the *status quo* and the American way of life—which is why there will probably be more people in churches on Mother's Day than on Pentecost.

But get to the crucifixion and the resurrection and we are at the heart of the matter; even if temporarily we are confused and don't know what to do with it. We are at the heart of the matter, mainly because it is our faith that God has done something in Jesus Christ that touches on everything from birth to death; which talks to us about real peace and love and brotherhood and freedom; freedom, not in terms of the Declaration of Independence, but in terms of freedom from the power of sin and death. It is a freedom not necessarily to "life, liberty, and the pursuit of happiness." When the New Testament speaks about freedom, it means the freedom to love God and neighbor as ourselves. And I can still hear the voices of those first-century Christians reminding us that it is also a freedom sometimes to be killed, to be scourged and brought before kings and governors for Jesus' sake.

Yet somehow in this faith in the resurrection of Jesus Christ there is power—even if it frightens us. We haven't really heard it if we aren't frightened a little. Even if it frightens us and makes us want to back away from it, there is power in it: the power that defied "dungeon, fire, and sword" and looked into the eye of the Roman Empire and Greek culture without blinking, without apologizing. Those first Christians just simply got up on their two hind legs and said: "We know something that makes Caesar's throne irrelevant." There is power in that if you know it. For this faith keeps telling us about the love of God overcoming—telling us that everything that says NO to us has been overcome and we don't have to take injustice and inhumanity as being forever in the saddle as just the way it is and sit back and dumbly fold our hands. And certainly it means that we don't have to go numbly toward death. There is power in that if it ever gets hold of us.

So we Christians are always having a continual conversation with ourselves about this faith. Now I know the charge is sometimes made that all we Christians do is talk to each other. "You don't *do* anything"—I've heard this so often. "All you Christians do is get together and talk to each other and then go home and that's the end of it." Well, I agree that if it's no more than that then it doesn't go anywhere. But we do talk to each other and we need to talk. That is what the New Testament really is. The New Testament is really a conversation; a conversation of Christians about this resurrection faith. You'll find it on almost every page. Here is Peter writing to his fellow Christians of the first century: "You know that you were ransomed . . . not with perishable things such as silver or gold, but with the precious blood of Christ . . . . Through him you have confidence in God, who raised him from the dead and gave him glory, so that your faith and hope are in God." (1 Peter 1:18, 21) Continual conversation—that's what preaching is all about, by the way. "I decided," Paul says, "to know nothing among you except Jesus Christ and him crucified." (1 Corinthians 2:2)

At the heart of the matter is the resurrection faith, and it infuses and pervades everything. Christian education is about this. When we strip away everything and get to the heart of the matter Christian education is a conversation about this faith— that the love of God has pierced beyond one's death and hell and the grave and that sin need no longer hold its power over any human soul; and, of course, that the love of God has something to say to the injustices of the world. Christian education is the transmission of this faith. Christian worship is about this. We worship in this faith, tell about it, pray because of it. We learn together how it ought to work on Wednesday afternoon at 3:00 when we are tired and come face to face with something that requires us to give notice of the fact that there is something more in this world than getting and spending—that there is such a thing as the love of God. Missions at home or abroad couldn't take a step without this faith, and social justice couldn't get off the ground without the power of this faith in a God who raised Jesus and said NO to every kind of injustice. And certainly the soul's salvation is about this. Soul salvation happens when we can really trust the mercy of God and can bring to it whatever dark thing is in our hearts. We believe in the mercy of God that once got itself seen in what the New Testament calls "the precious blood of Christ." (1 Peter 1:19)

Something happened called the resurrection. And what was once a shame and a shuddering and a hideous thing became a "glory"; thrusting itself toward the world, getting hold of ordinary people who find themselves doing impossible things, even sometimes seeming to be fools for Christ's sake.

So we keep talking about this, and we keep coming back to it, and we keep reexamining it. We talk to each other. We talk to anyone who will listen because deep down we know this is where the power is. Sometimes we get heard. People are converted and this "glory" gets hold of them. Sometimes we even hear ourselves. Then Christianity really comes alive and real commitments are made. Then a collection of names on a roll becomes a church.

But what is even more important, this faith becomes a personal matter and that is where the power really comes; as it did with two people on the road to Emmaus when "Jesus himself drew near and went with them." (Luke 24:15) He was alive, but that day it became a personal thing for them. They had heard about the resurrection, but they thought it was the talk of hysterical women and foolish men—it meant nothing until that day it became personal for them.

Sometimes this risen Christ—this Word of the blessed good news that God raised Jesus from the dead—can draw near to us and go with us—it really can. I can't say exactly how for you any more than I can say how the wind blows, but it does. Christ becomes personal; sometimes at the edge of things like disappointment, doubt, guilt, or grief; or when we've gone as far as we can go on our own and we know it and God knows it— sometimes when we're calm, just satisfied with human contacts and the social amenities that have neither depth nor height. Sometimes it happens, and sins are forgiven and disappointment is borne and grief is transformed. Prison gates are opened and there is joy and music and there comes a gladness—something more than just hope; and we pick ourselves up off the floor, and our flagging energies revive because he draws near. It happens. Sometimes suddenly, sometimes gradually, this Christ crucified and risen becomes personal and " 'our hearts burn within us while he talks to us on the road' " (Luke 24:32) and our eyes are open and we know *him*. We know the secret of power for the soul, know the Lord God who raises the dead; who draws near and goes with us and is able to deal with everything that we can bring to him.

The Christian faith is first about a living personal God— "who raised him [Jesus] from the dead and gave him glory, so that your faith and hope are in God." There is the power. The people of the New Testament on the other side of the cross knew it: "to all who received him, who believed in his name, he gave power to become children of God." (John 1:12)

Living with God's Freedom

All right. Maybe we are off the floor by now. Maybe we are still looking around, a little dazed. The next six chapters talk about what it means to live in freedom with this faith. Moses before the burning bush has something to say about courage and commitment. He asks us to believe some impossible things that have a way of accomplishing some very big things. Jonah gets in on the act and dares us to measure God. Then we bring it all back and ask if faith can touch our homes. And what about facing death? And there is also a chapter about believing in God's mercy and what we can do with that freedom.

*And the angel of the LORD appeared
to him [Moses] in a flame of fire out
of the midst of a bush; and he looked,
and lo, the bush was burning, yet it
was not consumed.*

Exodus 3:2; read Exodus 3:1–14

8

Rediscovering the Courage of Faith

We have come to a time in our history when all of us, young and old, need to turn again to the things that endure, to search for them diligently, to pray for them, to look at those things that build up the human spirit, those things that can give us real freedom for living.

For there are some things that continue to burn but are not consumed. Every generation must learn this or be consumed. Paul learned it on the Damascus road. He learned that something was alive that he thought was dead, and it changed the tenor and the direction of his entire life. Moses learned it when he turned aside one day to see why a bush burned in the wilderness but was not consumed. To the blessing of his time and to the blessing of the future generations, Moses said, "Why is this thing not consumed? Why is it not going out?" And he turned aside to see it.

And when he did, his name was called out of the bush and he was told that he stood on holy ground. The word that he heard was, " 'I am the God of your father, the God of Abraham,

the God of Isaac, and the God of Jacob.' " Now this was not a
pious formula. He stood on holy ground indeed, because Moses
was confronted with the faith of his fathers, the faith that he
thought was dead. It was a living thing; not shackled by time,
not consumed by skepticism, not worn out by the generations
of Abraham's descendants who had wept in Egypt in chains for
so long. It still lived. And every generation must learn this: that
the bush of God still burns, that a greater thing than themselves
still endures. Every generation is confronted with it. They may
turn away from it but every generation is confronted with it:
"Faith of our fathers! living still In spite of dungeon, fire, and
sword."

The bush of God still burns in his Church—still burns in
those of every age and generation who call upon the God of
Abraham who is the Father of our Lord Jesus Christ. Again and
again in history the wood has been piled high for its burning but
it has yet to be consumed. The bush of God still burns in his
Church; the Church in every age—the Church in every nation;
in small chapels and great cathedrals, in various denominations;
the Church, that ongoing community of faith. It simply will not
be put out or put aside. Despised, rejected, often in misery,
sometimes cowardly, but still that Church persists, with the
continuity of a great tradition in the best sense of that word;
even daring to hold within itself that which is its greatest continuing judge, the Bible. Yes, we can say that God's bush burns
in the Church, with its centuries of thinking, its proven disci-
plines and its sacraments which point to God. Of course, the
bush in the Church doesn't always burn brightly. But it does
burn, even sometimes on a dull Sunday morning. To rediscover
this is to rediscover part of the courage of faith.

Then there is the Bible itself. The Bible is not a collection
of proof texts, or something to be thumbed through as a kind
of magic book. It is to be read and heard as a recital of the
mighty acts of a living God from Genesis to Revelation, from the
garden of Eden to the garden of Gethsemane. Someone should
put up a sign: "God at work!" The Bible doesn't ask us how we
feel. It asks us what we are going to do, how we are going to
react to it. There is that old word from the garden of Eden story,

for example, that reminds us that there is something in us that makes us say no to God. We have debated about whether God created the world in seven twenty-four-hour days or not, and that isn't the point. We have debated about where the garden of Eden is located, and that isn't the point. The garden of Eden is in the heart of everyone now. Everyone has been created with the capacity to say no or yes to God. Or again for example, here is Abraham packing up his family and looking for something that he knows is better than where he is, something that is cleaner and finer and always keeping his eye ahead looking for it. That is what the Bible means when it says he is looking for a "city which has foundations, whose builder and maker is God." (Hebrews 11:10) There are contemporary Abrahams and Sarahs! Or here is one of the prophets, Amos, standing up and saying to the government, "We have become corrupt" and saying to the people who were taking bribes, "let justice roll down like waters, and righteousness like an everflowing stream." (Amos 5:24) The word of God does not stop to take our pulse. It says, "Here it is. How will you react?" This book talks about life and death and the soul's salvation, about neighbors and justice, about love that casts out fear, about our creation and our preservation, and if I may use one of the great old words of the faith, our sanctification. The Word of the living God continues to burn in this book. Again and again people have gathered wood to burn it. By their scorn or indifference they have concluded that it no longer has anything to say to the world. But it still is a bush that burns but is not consumed.

So when Moses stood before the burning bush, it was not just some kind of magic phenomenon—it was a deeper thing, it was a confrontation again with the faith of his fathers which had never gone out. Some things burn, he learned that day, but are not consumed.

But a word of caution to those who turn aside to see why this bush is not consumed—it always makes a claim: " 'Come, I will send you to Pharaoh that you may bring forth my people, the sons of Israel, out of Egypt.' " (Exodus 3:10) In other words: "Moses, join with me in my concern! Join with me in my passion for people, for what is right and for what is just." It was a giant's task. It was enough to rock a man back on his heels. It did rock a man back on his heels, for he learned that out of his faith, with which he was confronted again and which was asking him to say yes or no, there came a claim upon his soul. It was not just some petty thing. He had come in contact with unquenchable fire. He had come in contact with Justice with a capital *J,* with Truth with a capital *T*—but that Justice had gotten terribly specific! He heard God crying in the cries of a slave people. He had been hearing that for a long time, and no doubt stopping up his ears. Now he was safe in the wilderness, quietly keeping his sheep, but he still heard those cries. "Come and I will send you to Pharaoh." "Go down Moses, way down into Egypt land, tell old Pharaoh, let my people go." Paul met it on the Damascus road. He thought he was about the work of God, collecting Christians and putting them in jail or worse. And then there was this dreadful blinding light and this voice. And Paul the pious, Paul the churchman, Paul the man who thought he was doing everything necessary to satisfy God by going through the routine, was confronted with the God of Abraham and the father of our Lord Jesus Christ and he heard, " 'I am Jesus whom you are persecuting.' " (Acts 9:5)

This God who dwells in the bush is forever saying to anyone who gets close enough to him to hear it: "Join with me in my concern. Join with me in my passion. Join with me in my concern for wherever a person is treated unjustly because of sex or color. Join with me in my concern that there be justice in all levels of government, that people might dwell secure." Always there is this tension between God's word and the condition of people. We come into church and open the Bible and we cannot live in either very long until we are conscious of this tension: "let justice roll down like waters, and righteousness like an everflowing stream." (Amos 5:24) We are conscious of God's call to join with him in his concern. We are conscious of it every time we hear Jesus' story of the man left to die on the Jericho road—and of the only one—a social outcast—who stopped to help him.

I hope that from this generation will come some Gideons and Deborahs and a Moses perhaps, or a Paul—who see this burning bush and hear its claim. And I hope I will never get too old to keep on seeing it and hearing what it says and what it urges me to do and to be.

But one other word out of this bush: I suppose if we couldn't hear this word everything that I have said before now would create nothing but despair. And that is that the God of the bush is our promised help. Moses said, "Who am I? My God, who am I? That you, the living and eternal God, should call upon me to join you in your passion." And God said, " 'But I will be with you.' " (Exodus 3:12) This is the eternal dialogue between God and humanity. It kept the old prophets standing. It kept Moses on his way. David Livingstone, in deepest despair, still wrote in his diary that God's is "the word of a gentleman." And Luther, in the greatest passion and agony of spirit, but also in faith, was moved to say, "Here I stand, God help me." I am talking about faith in a personal God; faith in a loving and intelligent will, always working out within history and beyond history his own loving and sovereign purpose. "I will be with *you.*"

When Moses was an old man and stood to deliver his farewell address to the people he had loved and led for so long, there is a tender and revealing admonition. Moses bids them remember " 'him that dwelt in the bush.' " (Deuteronomy 33:16) That was the thing that had stuck with him; that day when he was confronted with the faith of his fathers and realized that it still burned; that day when a claim came out of that faith that took his whole life and set it on a new direction and he learned that no matter where he went and no matter what was going on, there was Another who was with him all the way. This God still speaks to every generation. Blessed is the person and blessed is the generation that turns aside to see why it is not consumed.

But it displeased Jonah exceedingly,
and he was angry. . . . And the LORD
said, ". . . should not I pity Nineveh?"
Jonah 4:1, 11

9

Finding the Freedom to Love

The idea of the universality of the Judeo-Christian faith began in the Old Testament; that is, the idea that God is not just the God of Israel, a private God, but he is the God of everyone. After Israel had returned from exile and were building up their country, many had a very narrow view about their mission. They thought that God was their own private property and was devoted exclusively to the care and feeding of Israel. The book of Jonah was written to rebuke this idea. And the book of Jonah is the story of one man's struggle to accept the fact that God's love extends to all of his creatures and is freely offered to all. The expression "being a Jonah" as we commonly use it means a person who brings bad luck, as Jonah did to the sailors on the ship when he tried to run away from his job. A great storm came up and they threw him overboard. But that really wasn't Jonah's trouble. Being a Jonah is something else entirely.

For one thing, Jonah had a message that he did not want to deliver. He really did not want Nineveh to be saved. God told him to go to Nineveh and say, "Yet forty days, and Nineveh shall be overthrown!" But he didn't want to give Nineveh even that small chance. He hated Nineveh, and with good reason, because Nineveh had been one of the ancient enemies of Israel. Nineveh had come with her armies and had destroyed and pillaged and taken captive; the Jews had good reason to hate these people and to want them dead. So Jonah is pictured as typical of the narrow-minded in Israel who thought God was their property and it was his business to bring their enemies to heel, not save them. This is the way it was in those days. One country had this god, another had that god and the god's business was to take care of the people in that particular country and to punish their enemies. (When they went to battle against their enemies, they were to be victorious.) But certainly Jonah knew that the message that God had given to him meant otherwise. I doubt Jonah really would have run away had it not been for that. I have never thought of Jonah as a man who was afraid of Nineveh. He just did not want to go to Nineveh. He did not want to deliver that message because he knew that if Nineveh were warned to repent, Nineveh had a chance. God meant to save Nineveh and Jonah did not want that.

Jonah wanted God to be as small as he. That is, he wanted a God who would destroy Nineveh; a God who would reflect the same feelings of prejudice and hatred and bitterness that he felt and not be concerned for them as human beings at all. And even up to the last minute Jonah hoped that God would be like that. Jonah preached. The king put on sackcloth and the people put on sackcloth and everyone prayed and repented but Jonah still got outside the city safely upon a hill and waited to see the fire and brimstone come down. When that didn't happen he was the maddest prophet you can imagine! He grew violently angry. Finally it came out. He had a conversation with God and God said, "You're angry Jonah." And Jonah said, "I certainly am angry. I came over here expecting to see you destroy these people and here you are saving them." And then he said to God in effect (the Bible does have a sense of humor!), I knew you were going to do it; I just knew you were going to do it. That's why I ran away to Tarsus in the first place: " 'I knew that thou art a gracious God and merciful, slow to anger and abounding in steadfast love and repentest of evil.' " (Jonah 4:2) What a way to drag a creed out of a man! But Jonah knew deep down in his heart that this was so. He knew it when God gave him the commission to go to Nineveh. Moses had said this to his people many years ago. When God came to Moses and identified himself, it was as " 'a God merciful and gracious, slow to anger, and abounding in steadfast love.' " (Exodus 34:6) Israel knew this. They should have known it because they, of all people, had already been recipients of that love. So Jonah said, "I knew it all along. I knew what you were. I just hoped you wouldn't be that way." He wanted God to be as small as he.

So then, God comes through here as a God of great mercy and love for all his children. That is the great message of the book of Jonah. "Should not I pity Nineveh?" God says to Jonah in effect: "Jonah, here you are. You pity this plant you are sitting under that came up in a night and perished in a night, and yet here are all these people of Nineveh ready to perish and you feel no pity at all. Well, you say, they are your enemies; they have done things against you and your people. But Jonah, do you really want God, sitting on the throne of the universe, holding in his hands all the power and justice, to be as small as you?" And then there is the question flung out to Jonah (the book of Jonah is the only book in the Bible I know that ends with a question), "Should not I pity Nineveh?" That is: Will you not *let* me be the God of grace and mercy? And Jonah is silent. Nothing more is said. The book simply ends with that question hanging there. He is silent, I think, because he is not willing finally to say to the God who sits upon the throne of the universe: Be as little and as narrow and as prejudiced and as vengeful as I am.

Now this part of the Bible may represent the best, and the most inspired thinking in Israel. It is the gospel in the Old Testament. The cross is in this book of Jonah; the cross with its message of sacrificial and suffering love on behalf of all people; the cross which in our faith is the symbol of what lies at the heart of the Creator; the cross that knows no boundaries. And Jesus said, not once, but several times, " 'many will come from east and west and sit at table with Abraham, Isaac, and Jacob in the kingdom of heaven.' " (Matthew 8:11) And even then, even though Jonah had preached the same message long ago, people were severely shocked by the idea that anyone could receive the blessings of God without going through the nation of Israel.

Once, when Jesus and his disciples were near Tyre and Sidon, a Syrophoenician woman came up with her daughter who was ill and begged Jesus to heal her. And an incident occurred that sometimes puzzles people. I think it is really not that difficult to understand. Jesus first of all refuses to do it. Then he says, " 'I was sent only to the lost sheep of the house of Israel.' " (Matthew 15:24) But I am certain that when he said that, he was looking over that woman's shoulder into the eyes of his disciples. He was challenging them—saying: "All right, you think I am only devoted to Israel; in your thinking God is only the God of Israel." The woman begged again and again and he put her off by saying, " 'It is not fair to take the children's bread and throw it to the dogs.' " "Dogs" was a reference to the Gentiles. The "children" of course were the Jews. But she said, " 'Yes, Lord, yet even the dogs eat the crumbs that fall from their master's table.' " He healed the daughter. It was a tremendous lesson brought home to the disciples that the God they were following was not a narrow, exclusive God, but a God who was concerned for all of his children.

Then there is the parable of the great banquet (Luke 14). The master of the house puts a feast on the table and then first invites his guests. When they refuse to come, he says to his servants, "Go out into the highways and hedges and bring anyone in who will come." And that is the voice of God: Should not I pity Nineveh or North Vietnam or Cuba or the draft dodger or that person you do not like?

Being a Jonah means being narrow and not free and open to everyone. Jonah was not free because his God was too small, his concern for himself was too great, and his love for others was too pinched and too reluctant. He could not be an evangelist to Nineveh. He could not be a missionary to anyone—just a prophet of doom who hoped that his prophecy would be fulfilled.

Dr. Helmut Gollwitzer, who was Professor at the Free University in Berlin, and assistant to Pastor Martin Niemoeller during the War, wrote this in a sermon which he called "True Freedom" (1958):

> The lack of freedom of the blocked door, the pharisaical self-justification, the anxiety toward the other, today rule the whole world. . . . The world cries today for nothing so much as for Christians, who are freed from this lack of freedom, who break with abandon through all the iron curtains, who recognize even in scoundrels God's beloved creation, who first ask in every case of enmity toward Christ where our own Christian lack of freedom may bear the guilt, who seek not to defend themselves from the Communists, but rather bring to the Communists God's love and freedom, who step into the cleft of the divided world and build bridges and perform the Samaritan service on all sides—without being concerned whether they will be misunderstood for it and reviled from all sides. In her history the church has been crippled again and again because she let herself be drawn inwardly into defensiveness, into self-assertion. Today, too, she is in this danger, and in many places the Christians are crippled in their service by anxiety and pharisaism. The fighting camps of the East and the West both want to put the church to their use. Wherever that is done, the church is unfree. She is free where she stands alone in the service of her Lord, who seeks *all* men.[1]

How big is my God? How merciful is he? Is he merciful enough to forgive my worst enemy? And the Communists? If I am black, is he big enough to forgive the whites that I believe threaten me? If I am white, is he big enough to forgive the blacks I think threaten me? Evangelism that does not have that spirit is not Christian evangelism.

The Christian faith calls us to serve and to proclaim and even, God help us, to *incarnate* a God of unmeasured love, one who always stretches our souls beyond all that we can imagine and will keep on stretching them until we cry out in pain; our faith calls us to stop living under the rule of our drives and our ambitions and our prejudices and even our bitterness; it calls us to be free and open and loving toward all people even as our God is. And this, I think, will be the pain of contemporary Christianity. With that pain under our souls, we may then become true evangelists.

Well, what do you think happened to Jonah under the impact of this experience? There was a historical prophet named Jonah. I can imagine that he did not go on being small and bitter and vengeful, but that his spirit grew as he learned about his God. Perhaps he became a true evangelist, and from that time on, he was eagerly willing to say to anyone shut up in any prison: "Courage my friend. Haven't you heard about God? He loves you. He is able to deliver you. His love is so great. He even forgave me." And when Jesus lay down to wait for the nail, surely Jonah was allowed to stand among the prophets and see it. If our God really is a God who pities Nineveh, if he really was in that act we call Calvary, then we have got a message and as the old spiritual puts it: "We've got a glory." The question is not whether we should have Christian missions or an evangelistic outreach. That isn't the question. The question is have we got a gospel big enough and free enough to love the world?

". . . he who made them from the beginning made them male and female."

Matthew 19:4

10

Letting God Touch My Marriage

"And the rib which the LORD God had taken from the man he made into a woman . . . . Then the man said, 'This at last is bone of my bones and flesh of my flesh. . . .' Therefore a man leaves his father and his mother and cleaves to his wife, and they become one flesh." (Genesis 2:22–24) "Wives, be subject to your husbands, as to the Lord. . . . Husbands, love your wives, as Christ loved the church. . . . Even so husbands should love their wives as [they love] their own bodies. . . . 'For this reason a man shall leave his father and mother and be joined to his wife, and the two shall become one.'" (Ephesians 5:22, 25, 28, 31) "And Pharisees came up to [Jesus] . . . and tested him by asking, 'Is it lawful to divorce one's wife for any cause?' He answered, 'Have you not read that he who made them from the beginning made them male and female, and said, "For this reason a man shall leave his father and mother and be joined to his wife and the two shall become one"? So they are no longer two but one. What therefore God has joined together, let no man put asunder.'" (Matthew 19:3–6)

"Dearly beloved, we have come here to join this man and this woman in holy matrimony." Holy Matrimony! With an exclamation point! A subject, I might say, with which I have had some experience, thirty years of experience to be precise. Now, any man has to be credited with some courage for undertaking to speak or write on this subject, especially if he is married, knowing full well that anything he says may be taken down as evidence and used against him! But blessed with a wife who has put up with more than her full share, and trusting in your good humor, I can hope to be read with some tolerance.

The Bible at least knows more than I do. And it says enough so that we may all profit from its wisdom. Most wedding ceremonies quote part of these words of Jesus in Matthew 19:4–6: " 'Have you not read that he who made them from the beginning made them male and female, and said, "For this reason a man shall leave his father and mother and be joined to his wife, and the two shall become one"? So they are no longer two but one. What therefore God has joined together, let no man put asunder.' "

Now, first, simply but definitely, this is saying that when a man and woman are married to each other, from that day forward *their first loyalty begins and ends with each other.* Whenever the minister pronounces the benediction and the recessional begins, from that moment on they form a new unit in society, and from that moment on their first loyalty is to each other; no matter where they are; no matter to whom they may be talking. Now this demands a maturity which some are not able to give even at 30 or 40 years of age. There are some men who simply cannot leave their fathers and mothers. There are some women who simply cannot leave their fathers and mothers. When the Bible says, "and be joined to his wife" or *vice versa* "and be joined to her husband," it means precisely to give your first loyalty to that person from this moment on.

So this question about being old enough for marriage doesn't have to do with numbers necessarily. I would concede that perhaps it is possible to do this, to have this kind of maturity, at the age of 19, but I rather doubt it. And the point is not whether we are old enough to beget children, but whether we are mature enough to give our first loyalty to another human being "in sickness and in health, in plenty and in want, in joy and in sorrow, till death do us part."

Now this is something we must all remember, including mothers- and fathers-in-law. I am now a father-in-law and I can see things from that side of the fence. Put simply and plainly, my dear fellow in-laws, this means that it is none of our business from that day on how she keeps the house, what he makes, and how they rear the children. There comes a time when we parents have to retire from the job. And I can tell you that is very difficult to do. Many strains and difficulties in marriage are created by the fact that we parents are not willing to retire.

"A man shall leave his father and mother and be joined to his wife." And probably the real measure of success in a marriage is: can we do this "in sickness and in health, in plenty and in want"? Not: how much money have we made? or what social status in the community have we achieved? or is our home spic and span, spotless from top to bottom, appointed with the latest furniture? No, our measure is this: have we been able to give our first loyalty to another human being "in sickness and in health, in plenty and in want"? Many marriages are simply being driven apart by lust on the part of one partner or the other for either making money or achieving social status; and in the process, forgetting that their first loyalty is to each other; and forgetting that when all is said and done, when all is made and lost, all they have is each other. "A man shall leave his father and mother and be joined to his wife." This is fundamental; it's absolutely basic; and no one has any business getting married until he or she is mature enough to do precisely that.

Also in marriage there is a joining of two human beings: "So they are no longer two but one." Now this is something far more than a physical joining. There is something spiritual and emotional here; the giving and receiving of *compassion* with one another, which no other human being in the world can give. It is "in sickness and in health, in plenty and in want" when we stand and walk together, when we travel the hard places as well as the smooth places together. No other human being can give the kind of compassion that a husband and wife can give to one another.

Some wedding ceremonies ask, "Do you promise to bear with each other's infirmities and weaknesses?" Part of being mature is to realize that we all have infirmities and weaknesses. Nothing is 100% in this world. If you are looking for 100% and decide that you will change partners and try to find it in another, you are going to fail. You will always have "to bear with each other's infirmities and weaknesses." Paul reminds us in 1 Corinthians 13 that real love is "patient and kind, . . . not jealous or boastful, . . . bears all things, believes all things, hopes all things." It may come as a surprise, but we do marry each other as human beings and not as angels. You may think that that fellow is the handsomest thing that ever came down the road. He just must be practically perfect. No, he's not! And you may believe that that young lady is practically sprouting wings and will almost momentarily take off and fly into the sunset. No, she won't. We are human beings. We are not angels. This is true of every one of us. We have our faults and failings, our "infirmities and weaknesses."

We marry each other as human beings not as angels. Presumably the Lord will make us that one day; but as long as we are on this earth we are human beings with our faults and failings. Marriage is the joining of two human beings in compassion; and also the joining of two human beings in *communication*. We marry each other as human beings who can talk to each other, who can express feelings to each other, so we ought to be able to talk to one another. This is important; this is very important, believe me. I suppose that this is one of the greatest mistakes that we make. We do not talk to our spouses nearly as much as we should. Involved in our work, by evening we are beaten and tired perhaps; when we see each other we simply find it difficult to get out another word. But communication is important; so often it is not the big things that cause marriages to go on the rocks, but many little things failing to be remedied for lack of communication. This "fable" often told has a "bite" in it: A man and a woman met one day at a party and they started talking. They discovered that each one was married; each had two children, a boy and a girl; each lived on the same street, with the same house number; and then they discovered that they were married to each other! Perhaps the greatest psychiatry that can take place in marriage is communication between two human beings who recognize each other's "infirmities and weaknesses," who love each other in spite of it, and who are ready to forgive and love each other.

Now the following has no relevance whatsoever except to Christians: marriage is a joining of two human beings in Jesus Christ. As Paul wrote to the Ephesians, "Husbands, love your wives, as Christ loved the church . . . and let the wife see that she respects her husband." "Wives, be subject to your husbands." (Ephesians 5:22, 25, 33) This does not mean that husbands are to be tyrants, nor does it mean that women are to play any type of subordinate role in marriage. Read the entire passage (Ephesians 5:21–33) carefully. Paul is talking to Christians and this has no meaning except to people who believe in Jesus Christ as Lord and Savior. In the marriage relationship, we Christian husbands and wives are to be subject to one another *as to the Lord.* "Husbands, love your wives, *as Christ loved* the church." "Wives, be subject to your husbands, *as to the Lord.*" There is no room for tyranny here or submission, but a great responsibility; a great responsibility particularly upon husbands. "Love your wives, as Christ loved the church" and gave himself up for her. And then Paul goes on in that great picture to compare the Church as the bride of Christ. Christ presents the Church to himself "without spot or wrinkle." So Paul in effect says to Christian husbands: "You are to love your wife as your own flesh. To nurture her, to take care of her, to be responsible for her, to love her, so that she might always be presented before you as a bride 'without spot or wrinkle.' " Even though the wrinkles come with the years, inside there won't really be any! "Husbands, love your wives, as Christ loved the church . . . and let the wife see that she respects her husband." And I think that it ought to be said that if a man does not do that, then he has lost the respect of his wife.

When we marry in the Church, we marry as Christians; and it is more than just a legal ceremony. It is the joining of two people in faith and in responsibility. To marry and live in the grace of Christ and in the love of God makes a Christian marriage. Who hasn't failed somewhere? Who is not in need of forgiveness and compassion such as Christ exhibited for the Church? We husbands need it; wives need it.

Calvin Coolidge is said to have paid a beautiful tribute to his wife, Grace: "For almost a quarter of a century now she has borne with my infirmities and I have rejoiced in her graces." We marry human beings. Marriage is the joining of two human beings in compassion, in communication, and in Jesus Christ.

One other thing: There is a third most important Person at every marriage. "He who made them from the beginning made them male and female," said Jesus. "What therefore God has joined together, let no man put asunder." The opening part of one wedding ceremony reads: "Dearly beloved, we are assembled here in the presence of God to join this Man and this Woman in holy matrimony; which is *instituted of God*, regulated by His commandments, blessed by our Lord, Jesus Christ, and to be held in honor among all men. Let us therefore reverently remember that God has established and sanctified marriage." (*The Book of Common Worship*, p. 183, italics added) This is what is holy about matrimony: it is done in the presence of God, who has established marriage. In addition to the ushers and the bridesmaids and the father of the bride, uncomfortable in his stiff collar and with his now sparse bank account, there is also a third Person. He is not a guest, but the establisher and the sanctifier of a worship service. It is not just a ceremony, but is "in the presence of God." Candles and flowers are beautiful, but if this faith is not present, the man and the woman are simply saying words. If they are not being said to God, who they believe establishes and sanctifies their marriage and their home, then a church wedding means nothing more than that a ceremony is being held in a building called a church. There is an indispensable triangle in marriage; the best kind of triangle: it is God at the top and the man and the woman at the bottom. And builders tell me that the triangle is the one single strong building unit of most buildings, particularly bridges—God at the top and the man and the woman at the bottom looking up to him.

In one wedding ceremony we promise "to pray for and encourage each other in the things which pertain to God." And these are also not just pious words. They mean that if we do not have Church and prayer and worship and Bible and God built somewhere into our homes and marriages, there will be, thereafter, a strength lacking that all the money and all the social position in the world cannot give "in sickness and in health, in plenty and in want, in joy and in sorrow, as long as we both shall live." "What therefore *God* has joined together."

"Do you take this man? Do you take this woman and pledge your troth in all love and honor, in all duty and service, in all faith and tenderness, as long as you both shall live?" I suppose this is life's greatest contract. Its strength sometimes seems to be such a fragile thing—seeing that we are all flesh and blood. But if it has any strength, that strength comes from two human beings giving their first loyalty to each other, forgiving and loving one another every day. Its joy is never in banks but in the shared laughter and the shared pain and the shared compassion. Its holiness is that it is offered to the God who gave it.

And now abideth faith, hope, love.
1 Corinthians 13:13 (KJV)

11

Where Does Faith Touch My Home?

Can faith touch my home? I know that one can ask that same question in connection with half a dozen other things. Where does faith touch my work and so on? But where does the Christian faith touch my home? That is, the Christian faith that God has freed us in Jesus Christ, has forgiven us, has restored us to himself and calls us now to be his children. Where does *this* freedom touch my home? Where does it touch my relationship with my wife or my husband or my children or my in-laws or whoever is within the place that I call home?

In the first place, the Christian faith touches the home in the Christian understanding of human nature. That is to say, we are not by nature "good." We are creatures of a broken relationship. We are creatures of a broken relationship with our maker. I have read many definitions of "original sin." One man said, "You never understand original sin until you have children!" Children might reverse that and say, "You never understand original sin until you have parents." But regardless of that, when we are honest with ourselves we know good and well that we are not perfect people, we are imperfect people. There are no perfect parents. There are no perfect children. There are no perfect husbands and no perfect wives. Of course, that can be carried too far. A few years ago I remember, when our children were growing up, one of the expressions among the young people was "nobody's perfect." Johnny comes home and his mother says, "Johnny, you didn't carry out the garbage, you didn't tell me where you were going and you have been gone for three hours; you didn't brush your teeth this morning and you didn't study your lessons." Johnny shrugs his shoulders and says, "Well, nobody's perfect!" We are, of course, imperfect. We are creatures of broken relationships, with no exceptions, in need of the "grace" of God. Not just my wife, but me. Martin Luther, writing about his wife, said, "I would not exchange Katie for France or Venice, because God has given her to me, and besides other women have worse faults!" Katie's remark has never been recorded! I think in the Christian understanding of human weakness the Christian faith ought to touch our homes—that there ought to be times, and I suspect those times are almost every day, when husbands should look at wives and wives should look at us husbands and we should all remind ourselves that we are fallible creatures, and we are in need of grace.

The Christian faith touches the home in the Christian belief in grace—that is, forgiveness, belief in the possibility of forgiveness, belief in the fact, first of all, that you and I have been forgiven by the sheer grace of God and nothing else. We didn't do a thing to earn it and we never will. God first loved us. Even before we were born, God sent his only Son. We fall out of relationship with God, we fall out of relationship with ourselves and with each other, and then there follows hostility and loneliness and alienation, which can only be healed by one thing: the mutuality of forgiving and serving love. "Perfect love casts out fear." (1 John 4:18) And we are all creatures of fear at one time or another: fear because of what we have done or what we haven't done; fear because we haven't lived up to something in the sight of our husbands or wives. And we can go at one another with our fists doubled up and with our hostilities riding rampant. Or we can go at one another and remember that by the grace of God we are his children, and that a doubled-up fist is always met by a doubled-up fist, but an opened hand is met by an opened hand. It's an old cliché, but it is still true: a doubled-up fist never built anything, but an open hand has immense possibilities. "Love suffereth long and is kind" says I Corinthians 13:4 in the King James translation. But in the words of this more modern translation, a feeling of mutuality of bearing and of compassion comes through: "Love is patient and kind; love is not jealous, or conceited, or proud; love is not ill-mannered, or selfish, or irritable; love does not keep a record of wrongs; love is not happy with evil, but is happy with the truth. Love never gives up: its faith, hope, and patience never fail." *(Good News for Modern Man)* If a married couple remembered nothing else, that would be enough. If we remembered nothing else, all of us, whether in our husband-and-wife relationship or in any of our other human relationships—if we remembered that, no doubt it would overcome many, many things.

The Christian faith touches the home in the Christian idea of "things." We all know that we live in a materialistic civilization. That is not to condemn material things; we all benefit from them. But, of course, the curse of a materialistic civilization is the tyranny of things. We are all under it in one way or another. Our children are born into it and we are bombarded by radio and television almost 24 hours a day. We are told, "If you don't have this thing, you can't be happy. If you don't brush your teeth with this kind of toothpaste, you won't get married." Who can ever forget a few years ago, that tragic TV commercial and that forlorn young lady who stepped before the camera and announced that her class did not brush with a certain kind of toothpaste and therefore got 37% fewer boyfriends! We are told, "If you don't drive this kind of car, then all the neighbors in the block will look down on you." Well, we know this. Sometimes we don't stop to think about what is being sold to us, but we know this. And "things" can dominate a home, its motives and its values. That is where problems come.

I remember a few years ago among young people there was

a label craze. All their clothes had to have the label of a certain store, or they simply weren't "dressed." Some people even went to the extent, I understand, of sewing phony labels into their clothes. And then there was a Madras shirt stage. I had hardly gotten past that stage when I discovered there was something else. So I decided to check up. You know, we preachers are supposed to keep up with everything and I thought I would find out what the latest fad was so I could mention it from the pulpit and all the young people would think I was really "with it." So I said to one of the young ladies in the church, "What are you all talking about now? What's the latest fad? What's the latest craze?" And she looked at me a little blankly and I said: "I mean, what are you all talking about now?" "Oh," she brightened up and said, "we talk about the boys and they talk about the girls!" And I stopped my research at that point.

The truth is that things can dominate us. They can dominate us as young people. And we can get the idea that if I just don't have this "thing" my life is awful, and will be ruined from now on and my parents are awful too. And before we parents begin to pat our feet and clap our hands about the young people, let's stop and think about the things that *we've* just *got* to have, and if we don't have them, we are failures. Things can become a pitiful substitute for love and understanding in the home. In spite of all the "things" in a home, there can still be hostility and tension and unhappiness. The prophet Amos once dared to speak out against the women who said to their husbands, " ' "Bring that we may drink!" ' " (Amos 4:1) But on the other hand, we husbands can fall into the same error and decide that the main thing in life is to get ahead. And one day we get ahead and we look around and where are our wives, our children? Where is the love and understanding that we should have been building up and didn't? And all the money we made and all the things we achieved and all the places we went, couldn't bring that back. We all need to learn what this means and we all need to keep it in mind. Jesus said it: " 'a man's life does not consist in the abundance of his possessions.' " (Luke 12:15)

Maybe the most valuable thing in the world right now is the face of your wife or husband and the love and devotion that has been given to you all these years; and if not husbands and wives, then those children that have been given to you; or that person who is particularly close to you in a human relationship. Are things more important than principles? Is society and status more important than achieving love and understanding? Is having things more important than having each other?

One other thing. The Christian faith ought to touch the home with faith itself. "Now abideth faith, hope, love, these three." There should be faith and hope in the home, the faith, for example, that breathes in that old story of Hannah and Elkanah when little Samuel was taken to the temple. Hannah said to Eli, " 'I am the woman who was standing here in your presence, praying to the LORD. . . . I prayed [to have this child]; and the LORD has granted me my petition . . . . Therefore I have lent him [the child, Samuel] to the LORD; as long as he lives, he is lent to the LORD.' " (1 Samuel 1:26–28) In that old story there is a kind of basic faith in God that ought not to be lost. Is it too old-fashioned? Has it gone out of date? Is it too old-fashioned for parents to pray to God for their children and to pray that they will be children for the Lord? The Bible says that in those days of Hannah and Elkanah and Samuel, "the word of the LORD was rare in those days; there was no frequent vision." (1 Samuel 3:1) What that means is that religion had fallen on evil days and there weren't many people paying any attention to worship and prayer to God. But there was Hannah praying that she might have a son for the Lord, and she did. And you and I live in a time when religion has fallen on evil days. When there are far more who will not pay attention to Bible and prayer and church than those who will. And there is no "frequent vision." Without apology I suggest that the time is well upon us for praying fathers and mothers who will not only pray that their children will be happy and successful (we all want that for our children and there is nothing wrong with that), but who will pray that they will be men and women for the Lord.

There should be faith and hope in the home; love yes, but also faith and hope. And perhaps this is the greatest inheritance that we can give our children: that it will be our faith before our children that the darkness of this world has no final victory, that regardless of all the prophets of darkness and doom, we walk as though the darkness has no final victory. So we build and so we work and so we pray, and one day we shall go home to our Father, but we shall have said to our children that the darkness never wins. There is no greater heritage to leave than that. We shall give them something priceless if our posture before them is not one of quavering, if we conduct all our affairs as though there is another world. It means to live *this* faith: "Yea, though I walk through the valley of the shadow of death, I will fear no evil, for thou art with me." (Psalm 23:4, KJV) It means to live *this* faith: "God is our refuge and strength . . . . Therefore we will not fear, though the earth be removed, and though the mountains be carried into the midst of the sea . . . The LORD of hosts is with us; the God of Jacob is our refuge." (Psalm 46:1, 2, 7, KJV) I would like to leave that faith with my children, for with it, I believe they shall need no other star.

"Blessed are the merciful for they shall obtain mercy."

Matthew 5:7

12

Helping Others to Be Human

"He also told this parable to some who trusted in themselves that they were righteous and despised others: 'Two men went up into the temple to pray, one a Pharisee and the other a tax collector. The Pharisee stood and prayed thus with himself, "God, I thank thee that I am not like other men, extortioners, unjust, adulterers, or even like this tax collector. I fast twice a week, I give tithes of all that I get." But the tax collector, standing far off, would not even lift up his eyes to heaven, but beat his breast, saying: "God, be merciful to me a sinner!" I tell you, this man went down to his house justified rather than the other; for everyone who exalts himself will be humbled, but he who humbles himself will be exalted.' " (Luke 18:9–14)

We talk sometimes about repentance, and we should. All of us need to do a lot more than we do. And probably there is more of the Pharisee in us than the publican or the tax collector. But it's not just enough to go around saying, "God, be merciful to me a sinner." Indeed there is a danger in this: just repenting and crying for mercy and pointing to our sins and crying for mercy and no more; actually making a cult out of being bad and always telling God about it. I have to agree with William Muehl of Yale, who calls this sort of person "the sophisticated sinner, reveling in divine love and tempted to make a ritual of self-discovery."[1] That can happen. We keep on "discovering" our sins. We keep on saying, "God, be merciful to me a sinner"— keep the revival meeting going, as it were. As Karl Barth used to say, we offer "our little bit of despair" to God on Sunday morning, and we think that that does it for a week at least. It's even grown to a kind of popularity. Muehl points to the hero or the heroine in television or in the movies who is sometimes a repentant sinner but who always goes on being a sinner! In *The Music Man* the con artist with a heart of gold is the hero. And who always helps out Hoss Cartwright with the rustlers— "Miss Lillie," of course, who operates the town dance hall and saloon. But "Miss Lillie" goes on being Miss Lillie. The sinner went down to his house "justified" all right—but what happened after that? How deep did it go? Dr. Muehl observes rightly that mercy received does more than stand around with eyes lifted to heaven in an ecstasy of self-blame and then go back to cheating the customers or operating the saloon. "Forgive us our debts as we forgive our debtors" is still in the Lord's Prayer. And Jesus said, "Blessed are the merciful, for they shall obtain mercy." Forgiveness goes both ways. After all, what does it mean to be a religious person? It means, for one thing, being stronger than this Pharisee's negative self-righteousness; he could do no more than say, "Lord, you know what I don't do." So Jesus said: "Blessed are the merciful, for they shall obtain mercy."

Mercy carries its own creative power. It enters into the needs and feelings of people and really sees how it is with others. There is Tolstoy's famous story of the Russian noblewoman who sat inside the theater weeping for a stage character while her driver froze to death in the snow outside. One day as I was trying to write there was a terrible noise outside my study and a whole crew of electrical workers complete with trucks and loudspeakers and things that go up and down and noises were working on the light pole in front of my house. My first reaction was annoyance, they were disturbing my holy thoughts! My second reaction was: My goodness, my bill sure was high this month! Then I finally got around to looking at those men as men, and I began to wonder about the dangers that were involved up there and what they were doing and what their working conditions were, how their wages were, and as I kept looking at them I began to wonder about how it was with them at home, whether they were happy, whether they were sad. I began to look at them as human beings . . . But it took me a long time to do that.

Mercy enters into the needs and feelings of others on a one-to-one basis; it is slow to make up its mind on everyone, quick to give people the benefit of the doubt. Mercy doesn't use others as some kind of instrument. And not only that, mercy is a *doing* as well as a feeling. Mercy is an active verb. Yes, it stands against injustices of any kind, wherever they are; mercy can't stand them. Mercy stands against the vast cruelties of war. Mercy tries, too, to do something about the harshness of our penal system. The question is not how much does Christian mercy feel, so much as how much does Christian mercy do? "Lord, have mercy," said the blind man to Jesus, and Jesus just didn't pat him on the head and say, "I'm so sorry for you; I hope you'll feel better"; he said, "Receive your sight."

Mercy enters into the needs and feelings of people; mercy is a "doing." Wherever mercy can do, can help, can change, it does. And mercy remembers that there is something that ought always be salvaged in your heart and in my heart; that there is something worth saving here. It sees ourselves and others not as masks or routines or functions or reputations, or successes or even failures; instead, it sees something of the glory of God in each one of us—sees something of promise and power and possibility in each one of us and wants that promise and power and possibility to come out.

Now, I'm afraid that we "religious" people have sometimes been among the chief sinners in this regard. We've been too quick with our conclusions. We put people in stereotypes, we try to impose on people "right opinions" and "proper opinions," and we don't always try to see people needing help just to put their lives together again.

Mercy wants to help put people together again inside. If

you want to think about the positive, think for a minute about the negative. It is negative and destructive—hard-faced and severe—judgments on others that create a hard-faced and severe world. But mercy creates and restores and builds up. Apparently, our Creator himself decided that mercy was the way to deal with us rebellious creatures—mercy is consistently what he has showed. I heard a man on television say to a Congressional committee on amnesty that "the good Lord talked to us about mercy and forgiveness, but never said anything about amnesty." Apparently he doesn't know that amnesty means forgiveness; indeed, the legal definition is "an act of forgiveness for past offenses." And however we may feel about what ought to be done after amnesty is granted (there is, indeed, I recognize, the principle of breaking the law to be considered); nevertheless, in this too, we Christians do have to consider what Jesus is saying about mercy; especially as we consider the mercy we have asked for and received. Mercy looks upon the world with eyes wide open to its hurts as well as its joy, and is committed to seeing the best. Mercy blesses even those who persecute it, rejoices with those who rejoice, weeps with those who weep, tries to live in harmony with one another, not repaying evil for evil, taking thought for what is noble in the sight of all—never seeking vengeance, but leaving that terrible thing in the hands of God who is still wiser than we (Romans 12). God reserves judgment for himself, but mercy he allows us also to show.

"Blessed are the merciful, for they shall obtain mercy." Every once in a while the thought strikes me that perhaps mercy can't flow from God to us until it flows from us to others. And that unless we show mercy, we haven't repented at all. " 'For if you forgive men their trespasses, your heavenly Father also will forgive you.' " (Matthew 6:14) And that's plain enough, I think. Forgiveness goes both ways, creating and shaping beautiful things as it flows from God to us and from us to others.

Sometimes I wonder if on the cross itself—where our salvation was being worked out; where something tremendous, even cosmic, and in the final analysis completely unexplainable was being done—if that great creative salvation began at the moment when Jesus said: " 'Father forgive them, for they know not what they do.' " (Luke 23:34)

Living with God's Impossible

Now we are at the heart of the matter. The next four chapters deal with that splendid "pageant" of Christian faith, the coming of Jesus, Immanuel, which means "God with us." God in Christ crucified and raised from the dead! What does it mean to live with this? This impossible drama of God which calls us to blessing and venture—is it really possible that there is something in this world (and beyond it) that is not defeated? And is it possible to live with this faith and not be defeated?

On the evening of that day, the first day of the week, the doors being shut where the disciples were, for fear of the Jews, Jesus came and stood among them and said to them, "Peace be with you. . . . As the Father has sent me, even so I send you."

John 20:19, 21

13

Believing God's Impossible

Some time ago, astronomer Allan R. Sandage of the Hale Observatories in California announced that he and his colleagues have seen the "edge" of the universe. Beyond that "edge," they say, there is nothing. The universe is finite. On the other hand, I have a camera and the distance gauge on that camera says I can set it for 5 feet or 10 feet or 60 feet or even (it says) for "infinity." Now my camera cannot see that far, and neither can a telescope. But in the resurrection we are dealing with the gauge set on infinity. We are seeing, not with a telescope or a camera but with the eyes of faith, that the road now runs through the grave and beyond. "On the evening of that day . . . Jesus came and stood among them." Simply and beautifully put. The Bible is very sparing about its superlatives, preferring to deal in this kind of beautiful understatement: "Jesus came and stood among them."

And if the resurrection is true it means that all that Jesus is has broken through on the other side of the grave; which both blesses and frightens me. I suppose if it were demonstrated to me beyond a doubt that a man had been raised from the dead I would be amazed and awed. But I doubt if it would cause any faith in me. But this man Jesus raised on the other side of the grave, that is a different matter. All that he *is*, has broken through! For the resurrection is not the celebration of the rebirth of the spring about which our editorial writers love to rhapsodize. It has nothing to do with spring. It could have happened in the dead of winter with snow on the ground. The resurrection has to do with the faith that God Almighty raised up Jesus Christ. When the first Christian sermon was preached at Pentecost, the apostle Peter rose and the first thing he said was, " 'This Jesus . . . [whom] you crucified . . . God raised . . . up.' " (Acts 2:23, 24) Broken through on the other side of Pilate and Caesar, on the other side of entrenched privilege, on the other side of Peter's denials and even Judas' betrayal, broken through on the other side of everything! "Jesus came and stood among them." Something has broken through—all that Jesus is—the love of God that shone so clearly through him, and even to this day, after all the years, still shines through; the Jesus who cared so much to go to the cross; the love of God fiercely contending for the hopeless and the helpless. *This* compassion broke through. He who said peacemakers are the children of God and talked of mercy and forgiveness as being more important than great worship, and the kingdom of God as more important than things—the one who said that has broken through. All that Jesus is, *this* is what God would preserve in the economy of his kingdom and let everything else go.

"On the evening of that day, . . . the doors being shut . . . for fear . . . Jesus came and stood among them." The resurrection means that the love of God has broken through and *no door is forever*. The power and the kingdom and the glory belong to God. Indeed, it means that now there are great doors standing open and great winds of eternity are forever blowing through. And no door need stay shut forever because of fear. For the love of God has broken through on the other side. And Paul with his great God-given heart stood at the cross and then looked at the open tomb and then said, as it were, "I see it! I see it!" At the end of Romans 8 he says, "For I am sure." And this is the picture of a man planting his flag and saying, "Here is where I stand." Then he calls off that great catalogue of terrors, that catalogue of seemingly closed doors: "I am sure that neither death, nor life, nor angels, nor principalities, nor things present, nor things to come, nor powers, nor height, nor depth, nor anything else in all creation, will be able to separate us from the love of God in Christ Jesus our Lord." And the book of the Revelation says it simplest and best: God "will wipe away every tear from their eyes and death shall be no more, neither shall there be mourning, nor crying nor pain any more." (Revelation 21:4)

"The doors being shut . . . for fear." This speaks to any one of us shut up in some upper room for God only knows what fear. God only knows what fear has closed and locked that door, or what terrors we think are on the outside. "Jesus came and stood among them." The door wasn't shut. No door is shut. No way is hopeless; and the heavens are not brass over our heads. Not that I am promised that everything on the other side of my present fear or my present anxiety will be exactly what I want. But on the other side of it is the love of God, which has broken through. Now, no door is forever. No terror is complete. And it is not within our faith to believe the victory belongs to anything or to anyone but God himself. "The doors being shut . . . for fear . . . , Jesus came and stood among them."

And he said, "Peace be with you." All that Jesus is has broken through, all of the love of God has broken through to say "Peace," to speak that healing word to the deep places of our hearts. Shalom aleichem—"Peace be with you"—the common daily Jewish greeting of friend to friend, as we say, "Good morning," which used to mean, "God be with you this morning." I have a great friend in Honolulu, a Hawaiian Christian preacher. I am sure Abraham Akaka would insist that what Jesus really said that morning was "Aloha!" On the other side of whatever that locked door means to us, he says, "Shalom, Aloha, Peace." Remember, Peter had denied him, and he and the other apostles had deserted him. Still, he came to them and said, "Peace." So on the other side of my stubborn rebellions, my denials, and my fears, Jesus comes and says, "Peace." And John says, "he showed them his hands and his side," and he said three times, "Peace be with you." John Calvin wrote the lines of this gentle hymn:

> *I greet Thee, who my sure Redeemer art,*
> *My only Trust and Saviour of my heart,*
> *Who pain didst undergo for my poor sake;*
> *I pray Thee from our hearts all cares to take.*
> *Our hope is in no other save in Thee;*
> *Our faith is built upon Thy promise free;*
> *Lord, give us peace, and make us calm and sure,*
> *That in Thy strength we evermore endure.*

No door is forever. And Jesus has broken through to say, "Peace" and also to say, "As my Father has sent me, *even so I send you.*" "Challenge" is an overworked word. "Demand" I think is too harsh. But "summons" perhaps is the word: a call to mission; the only mission he ever really gave. The love that broke through on the other side of everything calls us to that same mission, never letting us sit still while others hurt, and while others need loving and caring, need deliverance from fears, need to know that God cares. "So I send you." Can we believe the "impossible" glory of it—the meaning and the hope it lays on life; God's Son walking the way of love through pain, beyond death, and light breaking wherever he goes? He looks back at us and says, "Won't you come?"

we have a building from God, a
house not made with hands, eternal
in the heavens.

2 Corinthians 5:1

He who raised the Lord Jesus will
raise us also.

2 Corinthians 4:14

14

Living after Death

But what about living after death? From very ancient times people have believed in some kind of life after death. Or else they have yearned for it. The tombs of ancient Egypt testify to that hope—the Greeks believed in life after death. Cicero said, "I believe the souls of men to be immortal." The Hebrew faith was somewhat mixed and vague about the afterlife—you will find very little mention of it in the Old Testament—but the Hebrews did believe in a place called Sheol, which was a place of the "shades" or the spirits departed, but without much form or substance. As far back as we can go, people do believe in some kind of afterlife or have some kind of hope for it.

Some call it selfish—to believe in afterlife or even to hope for it. Some say that we should just accept death as "intelligible" in the order of things, and let it go at that. But I think those people are few, and I suspect that most of us are not willing to let it go at that.

What about the Christian understanding of death? I know that the subject can be morbid, but at the same time, to evade the fact of death can also be a sickness. And we have tried to do that far too much in our culture. With all kinds of evasions our culture has run away from the fact that we are mortal and that we die. The Christian is neither evasive nor morbid. The Christian is joyful and positive. "If the earthly tent we live in is destroyed," Paul said—and it will be—"we have a building from God, a house not made with hands, eternal in the heavens." And this is our joy and our faith. "He who raised the Lord Jesus," Paul says, "will raise us also." And this is our Christian faith. But we do have questions—we all have questions. For example: What happens after death? What is it like? What about recognition? And so on. I want to write about living after death under two big headings, and then put two things at the bottom of the page, so to speak.

There are no periods with God. Ordinarily a period means "this is over"—"this is the end"—"there is no more to be said" —period. But there are no periods with God. "If the earthly tent we live in is destroyed, we have a building from God, a house not made with hands." And Paul says a little farther on: "we know that while we are at home in the body we are away from the Lord, . . . we would rather be away from the body and at home with the Lord." (2 Corinthians 5:6, 8) No periods. We commit the body to the ground and we are through with that, but the spirit goes to be with the Lord immediately. I stress that word immediately because so often I have the question put to me, "What happens immediately after death?"

No periods. Something is going on. Something has already gone on. Pliny, the Roman historian, who observed Christians in their practices and who wrote more about them than any other, watched them in their early days burying their dead. As he watched a Christian funeral, he wrote somewhat in wonderment that "They follow his body rejoicing, as though he were [simply] going from one place to another." Now Pliny was a pagan, but he put our Christian faith in one tremendous sentence that we need to recapture in these days: shouldn't we, in place of our elaborate and somber funerals, have a few trumpets and even a few drums? "Going from one place to another" —and to his cynical Roman mind this was an incredible thing.

They put the bodies of their dead on their shoulders and they walked through the streets singing. No periods—only a dash at the end. "What is mortal," says Paul, is "swallowed up by life." (2 Corinthians 5:4) Think about that. I think that is one of the greatest and most hopeful sentences ever written—"What is mortal," and think of all we can put under *that* phrase: the pain and the anxiety and the pressures and the troubles and "the thousand natural shocks that flesh is heir to" as Hamlet put it —all of this is "swallowed up by life."

Some people have difficulty with the phrase in the Apostles' Creed: "the resurrection of the body." It does not mean the resurrection of flesh and blood. The New Testament is very clear about this. "Flesh and blood cannot inherit the kingdom of God," Paul says (1 Corinthians 15:50). I think the simplest way to understand it is to think of it as the resurrection of the "person." That is, I will be I and you will be you. "This mortal nature must put on immorality." (1 Corinthians 15:53) "This corruptible must put on incorruption" as the King James Version says. "We shall all be changed" because "flesh and blood cannot inherit the kingdom of God." No periods. God raised Jesus from the dead and this is what gives the final meaning to life for us Christians. Easter is not a once-a-year affair for us, it is a continual thing. We believe in the power of a God who can raise the dead.

Yet we do ask questions: What will it be like? Will we recognize each other? What about those lives that have been cut short? The Bible gives us hints and suggestions which cannot begin to describe the infinite and eternal ways of God. But take for example that very simple word of Jesus in John 14: "Let not your heart be troubled: ye believe in God, believe also in me. In my Father's house are many mansions." (KJV) It means many rooms or many resting places. I remember when I used to read that I had a vision of Scarlett O'Hara's mansion in *Gone with the Wind!* As time went on and I looked at myself more soberly, I was sure the Lord wasn't going to prepare anything like that for me. Maybe a room and a resting place. Jesus says simply, "I go to prepare a place for you." I am content to let him prepare that place and make all the arrangements, just so my name is on the reservation list when I walk up to the desk!

"He that believeth in me, though he were dead, yet shall he live." (John 11:25, KJV) What does the word "live" mean beyond the grave? I don't have the words or the concepts to begin to describe that, and I don't believe anyone has who only has a finite mind. But in Revelation, chapters 7, 21, and 22 (which we often hear read at funerals) the Bible in incomparably simple language tells us the things that will *not* be there: " 'death shall be no more, neither shall there be any mourning nor crying nor pain any more.' " (Revelation 21:4) That in itself ought to be enough. No sorrow, no crying, no death, no pain. "No temple" (21:22)—we'll need no church there. No place where we have to go and confess our sins and our mortality and beg the forgiveness of God. "And night shall be no more." (22:5) Night is the time of the fever-tossed illness. Night is the time when we wake up and all of those things that seemed so small at 3:00 in the afternoon seem like giants at 3:00 in the morning. "And the sea was no more." (21:1) To the Hebrew mind the sea was the symbol of separation and it still is. If you have ever stood on the edge of an ocean or if you have ever had a loved one on the other side of the ocean thousands of miles away—you know what the Bible means when it says, "and the sea was no more." " 'And God . . . will wipe away every tear from their eyes.' " (21:3, 4) That ought to be enough. But then it goes on and says, "And his servants shall serve him." (22:3, KJV) That hints at tremendous possibilities! I certainly do not want to sit around on a golden cloud and strum a harp. My goodness, I'd be bored to death in five minutes. But this is a suggestion of the continuation of infinite possibility—"his servants shall serve him." Here is the life which he put upon this earth for so many years—perhaps threescore and ten, perhaps only twoscore or less—but surely the God and Father of us all who made this life and who we believe loves us does not intend that it shall be snuffed out in its potentialities, never completely known. "His servants shall serve him."

And the Bible suggests beauty, again in words that fall far short of the real description: gates of pearl, golden streets—we've heard about that all our lives—also jewel-encrusted walls.

Now what did the writer of the book of Revelation do here but use the most beautiful things he knew of on earth to describe the beauty and the glory of that other world—so why not pearly gates and streets of gold and walls set with jewels as we sing in the old hymn: "There's a land that is fairer than day, and by faith we can see it afar"?

Recognition? Why not! I will be I and you will be you, but I certainly hope you will be fixed up a bit better because when I recognize you I want to see you at your best! I, of course, will need no adjustment. If God is our Father—why not? Why not recognition?

The Bible suggests joy and newness and fulfillment. And there is a wonderful line somewhere in the book of Revelation about "harpers harping with their harps." Of course if I had written it (since I used to play the trombone) I would have said: "Trombonists tromboning with their trombones!" Now to me that has a ring to it, but probably only to me. The point is that the Bible simply says that there shall be joy and newness and beauty and glory and fulfillment. "I shall dwell in the house of the LORD for ever" says the twenty-third Psalm. "In my Father's house," said Jesus, "are many mansions." We can trust God all the way.

"Now to him," says Paul, "who . . . is able to do far more abundantly than all that we ask or think, to him be glory . . . for ever and ever." (Ephesians 3:20) When we give up our dead, we give them up to Someone who is able to do for them far more than we can ever ask or even think.

Now I said I wanted to put two things at the bottom of the page: anytime we talk about our hope for life after death we need also to remember that in the meantime, we have this life. This is not a "pie in the sky" religion. We are still called to faithful living, to bending our efforts to seek justice and love mercy. In this faith we are never content to live the old, old life, but every day to keep trying to live the new, new life—believing that "we are God's children now," as the New Testament says, "it does not yet appear what we shall be." (1 John 3:2)

The other thing I want to put at the bottom of the page is in these words of Paul: "we do not lose heart. Though our outer nature is wasting away, our inner nature is being renewed every day. . . . So we are always of good courage." (2 Corinthians 4:16; 5:6)

> *And when the fight is fierce, the warfare long,*
> *Steals on the ear that distant triumph song,*
> *And hearts are brave again and arms are strong.*
> *["For All the Saints Who from Their Labors Rest"]*

We live until we die—and with the faith that we can trust God all the way—every step of the way and beyond, believing that he knows no periods, and that there are no iron curtains between us and his love.

And between the throne and the four living creatures and among the elders, I saw a Lamb standing, as though it had been slain.

Revelation 5:6

15

Something That Is Not Defeated

Believing in the ascension of Christ? That's a lot to swallow even for Alice's Queen who could believe six impossible things before breakfast. The ascension of Christ is rather embarrassing perhaps for the twentieth-century mind. We do not think in terms of people going up in the air, unless they are on a Saturn rocket! I saw a roadside sign, one of those "repent" signs, which said Jesus was the first astronaut! On Mt. Olive they show the tourists the print of a foot in the stone which is supposedly the last print of Jesus' foot before he went up in the air. But we do say he "ascended into heaven and sitteth on the right hand of God the Father Almighty." One major window in a church I know is dedicated to the ascension of our Lord. It *is* saying something. The New Testament is saying something.

In the first place, it is affirming the sovereignty of God. We must "see" this picture in Revelation, chapter 5—and by the way, it is a picture. The book of Revelation deals in pictures, but these pictures are mere representations. They are not to be taken literally. They are to be heard for what they represent.

And this picture of the lamb standing among the elders and the four living creatures is a "picture" of the exalted Christ at the seat of all power, at the center of creation. The four living creatures symbolize all creation. The "elders" stand for all the redeemed people of God, and of course, the throne stands for the sovereign power of the living God.

The exalted Christ at the center of all power: "I saw a Lamb standing, as though it had been slain." That is to say that Christ and all that he is is not defeated, or more precisely, that God is sovereign. God did not send Jesus Christ—Christ did not "happen"—just in order to die and be buried. This loving and redeeming act of God we worship is not buried somewhere under the Syrian sky but lives at the center of all power and all creation.

God is sovereign. Perhaps it is an almost discarded notion in practice today—this idea of the sovereignty of God. We pay lip service to it, but we really think if there is any sovereignty on earth, it must be ours. We used to say, "Man proposes but God disposes." Now it is probably: "God proposes but man disposes." And we used to sing about God "whose robe is the light and whose canopy space." But now *we* can walk in space. But here is this bold affirmation of the book of Revelation and indeed of the entire Bible, the exaltation of Jesus Christ by God's sovereign power. Or as Paul puts it, "Therefore God has highly exalted him and bestowed on him the name which is above every name." (Philippians 2:9)

And this is the first thing we are saying when we are talking about the ascension of Jesus Christ. All other sovereignties pass. One sovereignty remains: the sovereignty that raised Jesus Christ. This is the cornerstone of the Christian faith—faith in the sovereignty of Almighty God, who raised Jesus Christ from the dead. "I saw a Lamb standing, as though it had been slain." This death of Christ, this atonement, this blessed love has been raised to the seat of all power.

A group of school children were brought in church and told about the windows. At the ascension window one child exclaimed: "Look! You can still see where the nail was in his foot!" The print of the nail, the thrust of the sword still in his side. That is, this act of the love of the redeeming God has been raised by God's sovereignty to the center of all creation.

Also, the ascension means that Jesus Christ gives meaning to life both now and forever. It means that Jesus Christ is our hope for life now and beyond this life. Remember the *Rubáiyát:*

> *Ah Love! could you and I with Him conspire*
> *To grasp this sorry Scheme of Things entire,*
> *Would not we shatter it to bits—and then*
> *Re-mould it nearer to the Heart's Desire!*
>
> *[Stanza 99]*

"This sorry Scheme of Things entire." And sometimes it seems pretty sorry, doesn't it? Sometimes we look at all the "dark" of the world and it seems very dark and broken indeed. And perhaps sometimes it is so in our own lives. But *we* can't grasp this sorry scheme of things entire and remold it to our heart's desire. There is One who can. So again, look at this picture in the book of the Revelation. There is the throne of God and in the right hand of God was a scroll sealed with seven seals. The scroll stands for the scroll of the world's history, past and present and future—this sorry scheme of things entire, even my own personal scheme on this earth.

Who can open it? Who holds the key? Who can give meaning to history, to the future, and to my own life now? Who can touch it with meaning and with hope? And the answer: "And he [the Lamb] went and took the scroll from the right hand of him who was seated on the throne. And . . . the four living creatures and the twenty-four elders fell down before the Lamb, . . . and they sang . . ., 'Worthy art thou to take the scroll and to open the seals, for thou wast slain and by thy blood didst ransom men for God.' " (Revelation 5:7–9) Love made flesh, unconquered by sin and death, *this* is sovereign now and forever.

Revelation was written because, for the first time, Christians were suffering persecution and death. And the oppressor —Rome—could not be stopped—Rome was all-powerful—at least that was how it seemed; yet the first thing Revelation told these people was that Rome is *not* all-powerful—Rome does not

control the future. In other words, it is not this present darkness, this present thing that seems to be set against the face of
God, that controls, but it is the very love of God, fully revealed
in Jesus Christ, pierced for our sins, exalted to the right hand
of God. *This* is the thing that controls the future.

This is the core of our faith. Human evil and the assorted
woes of warfare, prejudice, and injustice do not have the final
word. There is a loving and divine will and purpose and we do
matter, we human beings; and the loving purpose of God in
Jesus Christ now dwells at the seat of all power in the universe.
So we strive and work and love and seek forgiveness in the
belief that this is so, and we look beyond death in the belief that
this is so.

For this picture in Revelation is of heaven. It is a picture
in the only words that we finite humans can understand. It
speaks of streets of gold and gates of pearl, where there is no
pain, no night, no sorrow, no crying. Now and at the end of
earth is the sovereign love of God in Jesus Christ.

Moreover, the ascension of Jesus Christ and all that it
means gives continued mission to the church. " 'You are witnesses,' " Jesus said (Luke 24:48). Luke says that the very last
thing Jesus said to these men before he parted from them, the
last thing they heard, the last great enduring commission from
his lips, was: " 'You are witnesses' "—witnesses in word and
deed to the sovereignty of God and his love. This is the
"mission."

The beating heart of the Church lies here in this faith. Paul
says, "we have this treasure in earthen vessels" (2 Corinthians
4:7), but we *have* it! Sometimes the vessel seems pretty
"earthen," I know. But this gives us the courage to hold on; to
struggle even with the institutional Church; with whatever is
outmoded and irrelevant, keeping some things going that were
once baptized as sacred cows but are no longer. Even when we
see less love and compassion in the Church than outside the
Church, despite all that, the Church is still the holder of this
faith that God rules, that Christ is triumphant, that it is possible
for there to be love and reconciliation between God and us, and
among us human beings. God's way of peace on this earth is

always open if we will take it and no one need die the death of sin or the grave. So we witness. So we teach our children.

One more thing about the ascension of Jesus Christ, and the sovereign exaltation of this love of God: it gives us hope in prayer. Again from Revelation: "And when he had taken the scroll, the four living creatures and the twenty-four elders fell down before the Lamb, each holding a harp, and with golden bowls full of incense, which are the prayers of the saints." (5:8) It means that we are *heard* by that love which ascended to the seat of all power. We are *heard* by that one whose torn side and nail-pierced hands now hold the scroll of the world's history. "Who is to condemn?" Paul asks in that great eighth chapter of Romans. When we stand before the throne, who is to condemn? "Is it Christ Jesus . . . who is at the right hand of God, who indeed intercedes for us?" (Romans 8:34) So we hope in prayer to be heard by this "Immortal Love, forever full, Forever flowing free," heard by the heart of the one who wept over Jerusalem and looked upon the multitudes with compassion, as sheep without a shepherd. And we *are* heard—heard by the one who holds the scrolls in his hands.

"I saw a Lamb standing, as though it had been slain." The love of God is not defeated. By that faith hope is given, lives are renewed, sins are forgiven, and our way leads not to the abyss, but to that place where God makes all things new and there is no more night. Prayers are heard by an infinite compassion. John Donne wrote in the last stanza of his "Hymn to God the Father":

> *I have a sin of fear, that when I have spun*
> *My last thread, I shall perish on the shore;*
> *But swear by thyself, that at my death thy Son*
> *Shall shine as he shines now, and heretofore;*
> *And, having done that, Thou hast done,*
> *I fear no more.*

So God's Son shines and shall shine, and we shall not perish on the shore. Worthy is the Lamb to receive glory and honor and blessing and power forevermore. Something there is that is not defeated.

*The grace of the Lord Jesus Christ
and the love of God and the fellowship of the Holy Spirit be with you
all.*

2 Corinthians 13:14

16

Believing in Three Impossible Things before Breakfast

Remember in Lewis Carroll's *Through the Looking-Glass* Alice finds herself in this strange world, an upside-down, topsy-turvy, hardly-to-be-believed world. She is standing in the middle of everything, looking quite bewildered. When Alice says, " 'one *ca'n't* believe impossible things,' " the mad Queen retorts: " 'Why, sometimes I've believed as many as six impossible things before breakfast!' "[1] And I suspect that when we come to this matter of the Trinity—one God in three persons, Father, Son, and Holy Spirit—there are many of us who share Alice's bewilderment and wonder. We feel we have to join the mad Queen and just simply believe three impossible things before breakfast. It's not easy to think about it—many have just turned it off and refused to struggle with it. But it *is* the Christian way of thinking about God. We baptize our children in the name of the Father, the Son, and the Holy Spirit. We are married in the name of the Father, the Son, and the Holy Spirit. We say in the creed, "I believe in God the Father, his only son, Jesus Christ our Lord, and in the Holy Spirit." And there is, of course, the familiar apostolic benediction that we hear very often at the conclusion of things; it comes from the very last words of Paul's second letter to the Corinthians: "The grace of the Lord Jesus Christ and the love of God and the fellowship of the Holy Spirit be with you all." It is practically the only Trinity "text" in the Bible, unless we count the one in Matthew 28:19, Jesus' great commission to go into all the world and baptize in the name of the Father, the Son, and the Holy Spirit.

Now what about believing in the Trinity? We begin with Jesus—which is the right place to begin, which is where Christians begin when we talk about Trinity. "The grace of the Lord Jesus. . . ." We begin with someone we know, a person of flesh and blood who spoke and lived among us—not the hidden, mysterious, transcendent God whom no human has ever seen —the creative power that brought all this and more than we can imagine into being—the ultimate being, vague and shadowy and mysterious. We begin with Jesus.

We begin rather with someone we know. "The grace of the Lord Jesus." In other words, *we believe that God has a face.* Paul puts it this way in one of his letters. He writes of "the light of the knowledge of the glory of God in the face of Christ." (2 Corinthians 4:6) The Gospel of John says very plainly, "No one has ever seen God; the only Son, he has made him known." (John 1:18) "And the Word became flesh and dwelt among us." (John 1:14)

We look at Jesus—living and dying on a cross, speaking words to us, words that we still know and repeat often in our most devastating and poignant moments: "Let not your heart be troubled: ye believe in God, believe also in me. In my Father's house are many mansions." (John 14:1-2, KJV) We look at Jesus living and dying, touching people with healing and beauty and love. The Old Testament people were always longing for the time when God would be with them and so they spoke of "Immanuel" which means "God with us." So the New Testament gospel writers, looking at Jesus, his life and his death, his resurrection, said, "This is Immanuel, this is God really with us. God has a face. Whatever mystery there is at the center of the universe—and mystery there surely is—in Jesus this mystery has shown itself, we believe, enough for us to understand that at the center of all things is love."

And that brings us to the second part of this text and the second part of the Holy Trinity: "The grace of the Lord Jesus Christ and the love of God." Now Paul does not say the love of God "the Father." Paul said "the love of God." Sometimes when we pronounce the benediction or when we hear the benediction pronounced, the minister will slip over and say "the love of God our Father." But Paul simply says "the love of God." Jesus did call him Father, and he taught us to pray: "Our Father, who art in heaven . . ." In order to be truthful and honest about what the Scriptures are really saying to us about God, I think we must say that this love of God does not necessarily have gender. The point is that dwelling at the center of all things we believe is love. The Being who created us, who is pure spirit, who is neither male nor female, is love.

Of course, I know the problem here: how are we to believe when faced with the unanswerable questions that seem to fly in the face of the love of God? And there are questions. I run into those questions almost every day. The one thing that I have to say to all of them is this: I do not believe in a God who wills pain. I believe he permits it and I don't know why. Many times I cannot understand why. Many times I must stand mute in the face of pain, but I do not believe in a God who stands over us to thrust pain upon us. And I also believe with Paul that nothing, "neither death nor life . . . nor anything else in all creation, will be able to separate us from the love of God in Christ Jesus our Lord." (Romans 8:38, 39) Not pain or death or tribulation or distress. And as a person and as a pastor, I find myself going back time and time again to the eighth chapter of Romans where Paul talks about nothing being able to come between us and that love, and he lists a whole catalogue of things—death and life and pain and peril and sword and nakedness—and he says none of those can separate us from that love; that love will still keep finding us through that pain, to hold us.

We believe in the love of God. And if we wish to call that love Father and Mother, if we wish to talk of all the most compassionate and generous loving things on earth to characterize that love, then so be it. I wish the makers of the Apostles' Creed had put in one other article: "I believe in the love of God."

But what about now? How can we experience God now? Jesus lived and died 2000 years ago. The Creed says he was "crucified, dead and buried . . . The third day He rose . . . He ascended into heaven." This is the Creed's way of saying what we know—that his bodily presence was withdrawn from us. We no longer have him. So—the Holy Spirit, the communion of the Holy Spirit or the fellowship of the Holy Spirit. The Spirit is sovereign and uncontained and works when and where and how he will, but above all else, he is God dwelling with us. Jesus called him "Counsellor" or "Comforter," and that doesn't mean a pillow. The word *comfort* is from two Latin words meaning "with strength." Jesus also called him "the Spirit of truth" and Jesus promised that when he went away the Holy Spirit, the Counsellor, the Comforter, the Spirit of truth would come to be with those who loved God, so they would be empowered to go and witness to Jesus as the revelation of God and the bringer of salvation (John 14).

The *fellowship* of the Holy Spirit—the Greek word for "fellowship" is one from which we get the word "common." It also means to share—and it also means partnership. Think of the "partnership of the Holy Spirit," the "sharing" of God with us. Think of the fact that God becomes "common" with us. The mysterious, transcendent, unknowable Creator once for a moment let the light of the knowledge of his glory be seen in the face of Jesus Christ. He is still present with us by the "fellowship"—the partnership, the sharing—of his Holy Spirit; sometimes it is with comfort, sometimes shaking us and disturbing us, sometimes pointing the way, sometimes showing us a duty, sometimes standing beside us and bringing to our hearts something of the love of God and the grace of the Lord Jesus Christ. But in any event, it means that we are never alone, we are never isolated—"The grace of the Lord Jesus Christ and the love of God and the fellowship of the Holy Spirit *be with you all.*"

The Holy Trinity—no one in the early church ever thought

to make up a difficult doctrine and say, "Let's try to think up
something so difficult for people to think about concerning God
that they will be pulling their hair and shaking their heads from
now on." Not at all. It just happened. This is the way we experience God—this is the way they experienced God—and the
Trinity is our way of talking about who God is and what he does
with us and what he does for us. We are not asked to believe
three impossible things before breakfast—not really. We are
asked to believe that Jesus is, that his grace is real, that the love
of God is, and that the one who is telling us this inside is the Holy
Spirit—the Spirit of the one living God who sent Jesus and who
was in Jesus and who lives and reigns with the Holy Spirit, "ever
one God, world without end."

Now, of course, this doesn't say anything unless we accept
the option of *living* with this faith—"after breakfast" if you will,
believing that this is what lies at the heart of things: not a void,
not a faceless, heartless power, but God's love and grace and
communion operating and moving in the universe. Christians
are supposed to go out into the world from worship believing
this; and this is why it is most frequently used as a benediction.
It is not a period at the end of the service; it is saying to us: when
we go out, we go out with the grace of the Lord Jesus Christ and
the love of God and the communion of the Holy Spirit. So it is
important what kind of faith in what kind of God we have; and
this is what the Trinitarian doctrine and formula makes us recognize. We have the option of living as though there is this kind
of God. For how we think and believe about God is the most
important thing—it is the first thing and the last thing about
religious practice. For if we believe that the Christian God is
Trinitarian in that he is a God who is love, who loves his creatures alike and desires that none shall be mistreated, *therefore*
"social justice." If we believe his love became known in Jesus
Christ whose death and resurrection is for the sin of all, and who
is still known by the Spirit who dwells with his creatures and
keeps showing us the truth, *therefore* "evangelism."

He still lives, so we do not have to pronounce a benediction
on the world which might go something like this: "Now may the
power of the atomic bomb, and the security of things, and the

fellowship of prejudice and selfishness be with you all."

And our belief really doesn't mean anything unless it gets itself *done*—acted upon—unless it affects life—important decisions we make about money, human-racial-personal-male-female decisions that affect whether or not something good or something bad happens. Our belief doesn't mean anything—unless we are faithful to our calling to witness to this kind of God in the world where money, sex, race, and power call the shots —unless someone *acts* as though there is such a thing as the love of God and the fellowship of the Holy Spirit and the grace of the Lord Jesus Christ—"ever one God world without end."

Living with God's Courage

There is such a thing as living with God's courage; that is, the courage that comes from faith in the God seen in Jesus Christ. After all, in what kind of God do we believe? Not just "the Man upstairs"—but who is he and what is he like? We have been saying he is like Jesus Christ, that the love we see in Jesus Christ came into this world from God and is not defeated. There is a courage in believing that.

*the oil of gladness instead of mourn-
ing, the mantle of praise instead of a
faint spirit.*

Isaiah 61:3

17

Not Giving Up

How about wearing a sportcoat of faith instead of sackcloth and ashes? "The mantle of praise instead of a faint spirit." This is what this man is trying to say. We are with the Jewish exiles in Babylon and they are listening to the voice of a prophet-preacher we call second Isaiah bringing them encouragement and hope. He announces himself as having the spirit of the Lord upon him "to bring good tidings . . . to bind up the broken-hearted, to proclaim liberty to the captives . . . to give . . . the mantle of praise instead of a faint spirit." (Isaiah 61:1–3) Or a sportcoat instead of sackcloth and ashes! Why? Because God hasn't quit on you, says second Isaiah. I don't know why God doesn't give up. No doubt they couldn't figure it out either. When the "preacher" said that I imagine they looked around at one another where they had been for fifty years and more with their own homeland in ruins and said, "This is perfectly ridiculous; surely God quit on us a long time ago." God certainly had every reason to quit. Throughout history Israel had been "a stiff-necked people." They were people who had denied their heritage. They had come to the point where they had assumed they were God's pets and that no matter what they did he would take care of them—so when judgment and destruction came upon them they were utterly appalled and shocked. But now they had had fifty years of reflection and the more honest among them were disposed to say: "No wonder God has quit on us."

Well, how about now? Things seem "brown around the edges," to say the least. And it's all especially aggravated today by the prophets of doom who use the Bible to tell us how bad things are and how much worse they're going to get—how so-called prophecies of doom are being fulfilled and how the Lord is going to come when things get bad enough. But in the meantime, wring your hands, sit down and look sad! A man said to me with something of glee in his voice, "Don't you think things are terrible?" And before I could get a word out he said, "And they're going to get worse, praise the Lord!" And I found it a little difficult to join in praising the Lord for things getting worse.

Joey Adams, the comedian, tells the story about a theatrical agent who hated actors. His biggest pleasure was telling an actor, "Don't call us, we'll call you." Well, when television came along and there were no theaters for him to book, he suddenly discovered God and begged for help. God sent an angel down to see him. The angel listened to his lament and said (you guessed it), "Don't call us, we'll call you!"[1] Sometimes I think this may be the prevailing mood now. Maybe God has quit. Don't call him, he'll call us—maybe. Why not give up on those Jews in Babylon? Why not give up on *me* for that matter?

But God didn't give up—which is what second Isaiah was trying to tell those people: he has sent me "to bind up the broken-hearted, to proclaim liberty to the captives . . . to comfort all who mourn; to grant to those who mourn in Zion—to give them a garland instead of ashes, the oil of gladness instead of mourning, the mantle of praise instead of a faint spirit." "The mantle of praise . . . ." A sportcoat instead of sackcloth and ashes. "The mantle of praise"—the Hebrew word "mantle" is a very old word and not used very often. It was a word for the brightly

colored robe which the high priest put on over his other gar-
ments. It may have been the last thing he put on before he went
into the temple to offer sacrifices to God. "The mantle of praise
instead of a faint spirit." And who wouldn't rather have "the
mantle of praise"—except those who for some reason really
aren't happy unless they are going around with "a faint spirit"?

Gerard Manley Hopkins has a poem in which there are
these rather dark lines: "tell Summer No, Bid joy back, . . . keep
Hope pale."[2] Well, second Isaiah was saying, "Let's don't tell
summer No, let's don't bid joy back, let's don't keep hope pale
—God hasn't quit on us." Why? Why do we insist on that?

For one thing, we believe that his purpose keeps marching
through history. Which is what second Isaiah was saying: "For
as the earth brings forth its shoots, and as a garden causes what
is sown in it to spring up, so the Lord GOD will cause righteousness and praise to spring forth before all the nations." (Isaiah
61:11) He saw God at work in history with a purpose—working
like a seed sown in the ground—working with unlikely people,
like the Persian dictator Cyrus. Cyrus had never heard of
Abraham, Isaac, Jacob, or Moses, but second Isaiah saw God's
purpose working in him—eventually to conquer Babylon and
release the captives. God's purpose—it's the whole story from
Genesis to Revelation if you read it right. It never seems to give
up, always at work, right down to the day when Jesus of
Nazareth was invited to occupy the pulpit in his hometown
synagogue and read the sixty-first chapter of Isaiah. And when
Jesus finished reading it he said, " 'Today this scripture has been
fulfilled in your hearing.' " (Luke 4:21)

God's purpose marching through history. It is a purpose
made of love. "To bind up the brokenhearted . . . to comfort all
who mourn." God meant it—he did it for those brokenhearted
exiles. God meant it and he did it for all "exiles" in Jesus Christ
—to give us a second chance. Loren Eiseley, the anthropologist,
in his book *The Unexpected Universe* tells of walking one morning very early along the beach in California and looking at all
of the dead and dying creatures washed up during the night,
ringing the shore. He was looking at what had once been vi-
brant life now powerless, it seemed, to get back to the ocean for

a second chance. He came upon a stranger bending over a starfish. It was still alive. He picked up the starfish and "spun it . . . far out into the sea. . . . 'It may live,' he said."[3] That is what God in Jesus Christ has come to do for us—to give us a second chance to live. "To bind up the brokenhearted . . . to comfort all who mourn." "To proclaim liberty to the captives." It is a purpose made of love that keeps marching through history, reappearing, of course, every Christmastime with a beautiful burst of light and color, and a joy throughout the year.

It is a purpose that wants to enlist you! This may come as a shock. None of this business of sitting down and being sad and waiting for prophecies of doom to be fulfilled. This is a defeatist kind of religion and is not the kind of religion that is really in the Bible. The exiles could have sat down and said: "Well, that's it. Forget about the religion of Abraham, Isaac, and Jacob. Forget about our bright heritage. Forget about our mission." Instead, listen to the voice of second Isaiah saying to these people: "They shall build up the ancient ruins, they shall raise up the former devastations; they shall repair the ruined cities, the devastations of many generations." (Isaiah 61:4) Who will enlist in *that* purpose? That's what God was calling them to do. Get on your feet. There's work to be done. I have a job for you. I want you to be a part of my purpose and I'm going to release you for that purpose.

So everything is going to the dogs, is it? Are you in that crowd that is sitting around watching everything going to the dogs? Does it have to? Give up on the institutional Church, I've heard people say. No use having anything more to do with it. And they can find a hundred reasons why not and when they get through I can give them ten more. Give up on working for peace in the world—no use in that. Looks as though we're finally going to blow ourselves up. Give up on working for social justice—no use in that either—everything is stacked against it. Somehow the purpose of God keeps coming up to us and saying, "Shame on you—there's work to be done, will you join me in it?" How about "hanging in there" and wearing "the mantle of praise" instead of "a faint spirit"? For those who have given up on the Church I haven't anything but regret that they are staying out of the greatest adventure in the world. There is a Purpose that wants to enlist such adventurers in its ranks—promising hard work, mind you, but also a "glory."

Someone once asked Martin Luther, "What would you do if you knew beyond the shadow of a doubt that the end of the world would come tomorrow?" Luther is reported to have said, "I would plant a tree." "The mantle of praise instead of a faint spirit." It's not brown around the edges, it's green—green with the everlasting purpose of God—as green as a Christmas tree—a purpose that came "upon a midnight clear" and "angels bending near the earth to touch their harps of gold."

*So all the generations from
Abraham to David were fourteen
generations, and from David to the
deportation to Babylon fourteen
generations, and from the deportation to Babylon to the Christ fourteen generations.*

Matthew 1:17

18

The Years Are Not Empty

The years have a way of tumbling over one another and we
wonder where they went. More especially we wonder if they
contain anything of meaning—if God is really in them, or if they
are a series of events without direction and purpose. Does faith
really have any place? Can we believe that God is in events
working out a purpose filled with a sovereign love? Are the
years empty?

Enter this seemingly dull sentence from the preface of the
Gospel according to Matthew: "all the generations from
Abraham to David were fourteen generations, and from David
to the deportation to Babylon fourteen generations, and from
the deportation to Babylon to the Christ fourteen generations."

First, it suggests that what we call "Christmas" is not an
isolated event, something that just happened to take place with
no relation to anything that had gone before it. What had gone
before it was the "Old Testament": "from Abraham to David
. . . to Babylon . . . to the Christ." People ask, "Why bother with
the Old Testament?" We bother with it because without it

Christmas and the New Testament have no meaning at all. We bother because the Old Testament is like the roots of a tree. The preface to Matthew's Gospel and the agony of all of Israel's history, the wilderness, the conquest, the judges, the kings, the exile, and the coming back again, all of these things are part of the same story. The Old Testament rushes toward the first page of the New Testament. As the letter to the Hebrews tells us, "God, who at sundry times and in diverse manners spoke . . . by the prophets, Has in these last days spoken to us by his Son." (Hebrews 1:1, KJV) In one sentence the whole Bible is summed up: "from Abraham to David . . . to the Christ." And the Old Testament and the New Testament meet together above a manger.

And this reminds us of the faith of many people. There is a grand sweep of faith here—the faith of many people. The main thing that we ought to see here is people. After a long roster of the great heroes and heroines of faith, Hebrews 11 concludes: "time would fail me to tell of [all] . . . of whom the world was not worthy." "Fourteen generations" three times repeated. We look back with awe at these men and women who "died in faith, not having received what was promised." (Hebrews 11:13) And if we listen we might hear drums beating and trumpets sounding and see old banners raised. Great names stand out: Abraham, Moses, Joshua, Gideon, David, Isaiah. But think also of the unknowns, the unsung, the little people, who followed, who prayed, who taught their children to believe in God and to fear God, who lived in faith during the long years, who went away into the bitterest agony—into exile—and thought that the end had come, and who trudged back again to rebuild.

All of these people came to focus in one old man in the New Testament. His name was Simeon. He only appears on stage for a moment. Just for a moment the spotlight is thrown on Simeon, in the early days in the birth story of Jesus. Simeon going into the temple encounters Joseph and Mary and the child, and through some insight which only God can give, he saw in that child the fulfillment of the hopes of his people. So in that one moment with the light of God's knowledge and grace shining in his face, Simeon gathers up all the hopes and dreams and prayers of his people. Behind him there rises one by one all those greats and unknowns, as Simeon takes the child in his arms and says, " 'Lord, now lettest thou thy servant depart in peace, . . . for mine eyes have seen thy salvation.' " (Luke 2:29)

So the long years are in this text. If we are looking for drama, it is here—the drama of the little people as well as the great, the drama of many hands folded and many knees bent, many tears fallen, many hopes lifted against the day that God would visit his people. The long years, the faith, and the prayers of many people stood in company with the angel who said to Joseph: " 'Joseph, son of David, do not fear to take Mary your wife, for that which is conceived in her is of the Holy Spirit.' " (Matthew 1:20)

So there is here a call for faith—out of long years past. "All the generations." I grow very quiet when I read that. I think of the many stalwart men and women of the long past who speak to us out of this text: "the generations from Abraham to David . . . from David to . . . Babylon . . . and from . . . Babylon to Christ." Many voices, and if we grow quiet perhaps we can hear them telling us to gather again our faith and to lift up our heads. I hear the psalmist: "The LORD is my light and my salvation; whom shall I fear? . . . though war rise against me yet I will be confident"; "The LORD is my shepherd, I shall not want. He makes me lie down in green pastures . . . Even though I walk through the valley of the shadow of death, I fear no evil; for thou art with me; thy rod and thy staff, they comfort me." (Psalms 27:1, 3; 23:1, 4). I hear Isaiah: "Comfort, comfort my people, says your God. Speak tenderly to Jerusalem . . . they who wait for the LORD shall renew their strength, they shall mount up with wings like eagles, they shall run and not be weary, they shall walk and not faint." (Isaiah 40:1, 2, 31) "The people who walked in darkness have seen a great light." (Isaiah 9:2) We are called to faith as we listen to the old voices speaking to us about God and his ways and how we must learn to wait upon God and keep faith and how that faith keeps calling us to stretch our souls beyond anything we thought we could do, pressing us beyond that which we can see.

In the city of Ur, there was a man named Abram. On a quiet day he made a decision to go from his country and his father's house. When his friends and neighbors saw him going with all of his belongings someone said, "Where is Abram going?" And the answer was, "I don't know. He is off to wander I suppose." One day they called in a young man keeping his sheep. No one had ever thought much about his future. He was the youngest. He had several brothers who had far more promise than he. Besides, he liked to sing too much and compose poetry, and he was a bit on the religious side. But one day they called him in and old Samuel anointed his head with oil and made him king of Israel. His name was David. And upon a midnight clear in a little town called Bethlehem, a child was born in the city of David. While armies marched and kings planned and the mighty men of the earth thought they held in their grasp the kingdom and the power and the glory; but it was not so. The living God was working with people of faith and setting in motion the most powerful forces—*his* is the kingdom and the power and the glory. And so we go to Bethlehem and think quietly and deeply on this: that across the long generations God is with people of faith, that he has sent his Son as a pledge that this is not a forsaken and lonely world.

They say we are living at the end of an era, and the beginning of another, with more sweeping changes. Sweeping economic changes and reforms are predicted. The shape of world politics and world power is changing before our very eyes. The changes can be creative and constructive if we and Russia, for example, are willing to reduce arms, to recognize the responsibility of our technological leadership and turn our wealth to helping others in the world to rise. There will then be the possibility of "peace on earth, good will among men." But it will require a great faith and moral courage among those who believe in God's power, who believe in the justice of God and in God's purpose to bring "peace on earth." The energy crisis, and the fact that we are learning that we cannot fight and win wars while sustaining our economy, the Old Testament would say, may be God's way of plucking at our sleeves.

If we can hold to our faith in God and not yield to fear; if we can love God and neighbor as ourselves—these are still the greatest commandments for life; and if we can believe that Jesus Christ means that the love and the power of God is still at work in the world, then we shall come through as those who believed before us. They came through "not having received what was promised, but having seen it and greeted it from afar." (Hebrews 11:13) If we can do that, we can take our place among the company of those who stretch back into the ages, who loved and feared God, and who believed that his purposes would prevail. "We are not of those who shrink back and are destroyed, but of those who have faith and keep their souls." (Hebrews 10:39)

On May 11, 1659, the General Court of the Massachusetts Bay Colony passed the following law: "Whosoever shall be found observing any such day as Christmas or the like, either by forbearing labor, feasting or any other way as a festival, shall be fined five shillings." What a dreadful law. For Christmas surely calls for joy—not hilarity, but the deep quiet joy of those who believe that "from Abraham to David to Babylon to Christ" to the twentieth century, to the end of the age, God is our help in ages past, our hope for years to come. This is the joy that sings:

> *No more let sins and sorrows grow,*
> *Nor thorns infest the ground;*
> *He comes to make His blessings flow*
> *Far as the curse is found.*[1]

So this is our "impossible" faith: God is with us, not against us but for us; never removed in cold and silent isolation but present with all people.

> *O little town of Bethlehem, How still we see thee*
> *lie;*
> *Above thy deep and dreamless sleep The silent stars*
> *go by.*
> *Yet in thy dark streets shineth The everlasting*
> *Light;*

> *The hopes and fears of all the years Are met in thee*
> *tonight.*

The years are not empty—they are full of the love of God. We
live in this courage.

O that thou wouldst rend the heavens and come down.

Isaiah 64:1

Grace to you and peace from God our Father and the Lord Jesus Christ. . . . who will sustain you to the end.

1 Corinthians 1:3, 8

19

Someone for the Hurting

Well we have come this far together. Maybe the impossible is still impossible. Your condition has not been reached. You may still be tempted to give up, to live closer to doubt than to faith. (Incidentally, doubt is never far from faith, as love is never far from hate, so don't be ashamed of the doubt.) We may be hurting. We are all hurting somewhere I expect. And an honest prayer might be: "God, we're hurting. Where are you?" This was the cry of the old Hebrews in exile in Babylon: God, we're hurting. Where are you? "O that thou wouldst rend the heavens and come down."

I am sure this question comes in a variety of ways, but it comes. Where is God? It comes especially as we consider the anguish and suffering of so many people on this earth. I am also sure that it comes from those of us who feel ourselves, at times, far from God, living in a kind of "exile" of our own. We go to church—sometimes. We participate, we give, and yet there is this feeling of alienation. And it does not take a lot to experience this—a death, a domestic tragedy, an illness, a disappointment, or even some guilt for which we cannot forgive ourselves. These things and many others can put us in a situation where we are reluctant to pray, and probably we can get only this far, if this far: "God, we're hurting. Where are you?"

God must be angry with us, we think. As a psalmist put it who may have lived with the exiles in their concentration camp in Babylon: "Wilt thou be angry with us for ever?" (Psalm 85:5) They were there for their sins, so they had been told. Now they had come to the point where they said in effect: "God, are you going to crush down upon us like a tremendous weight forever?" The prophet who was with them in exile, second Isaiah, gives voice to this same thing: "The yearning of thy heart and thy compassion are withheld from me." (Isaiah 63:15) That is, "O God, it seems as though you are far away and your compassion is nowhere touching where I hurt." Have you ever felt this way?

Yet in all of this there is a cry—a holding on—a deep cry for God to come and to know that we are still here, just as we are, and hurting. God, would you please come and look at us? "O that thou wouldst rend the heavens and come down." Why won't you split the heavens and come down and look at us? Just part the heavens, the Mystery before which we all live, and come rushing to our condition. Do something! "Make thy name known to thy adversaries." (Isaiah 64:2) Wrong is walking all around us—getting and spending and having a great time, and it looks as though you don't care. Split the heavens. Maybe a legion or two of angels would do. Just so "they" would know: "that the nations might tremble at thy presence." (Isaiah 64:2) Rulers come and go. Great men sit on thrones and no one seems to care in heaven—or in hell. So they cried. But still they held on. They still said "Thou"—"O that *thou* wouldst rend the heavens and come down."

So throughout the hurting there runs the strongest kind of affirmation: "For *thou* art our Father, though Abraham does not know us and Israel does not acknowledge us." (Isaiah 63:16) We are cut off from our heritage, from our home—yet *"thou,* O LORD, art our Father, our Redeemer from of old is thy name." (Isaiah 63:16) I wonder if they were remembering the deliverance from Egypt—still a deep part of their faith; just as we keep remembering the cross? Did the memory of the deliverance from Egypt remain with them, still bringing its own power to strengthen the heart of faith? Is this what kept them holding on? Believing that the delivering God would come?

Well, he did come. He came into the hurting. No, the heavens were not split. Some said there was a star that night. And some said they heard angels. But he did come. He came into the hurting—all the way into the hurting. Paul puts it in a way that makes us tremble: "For our sake he [God] made him to be sin who knew no sin." (2 Corinthians 5:21) Then there are the old words from Isaiah: "he was wounded for our transgressions, he was bruised for our iniquities . . . . All we like sheep have gone astray; . . . and the LORD has laid on him the iniquity of us all." (Isaiah 53:5, 6)

He did come into the hurting; and he gives us gifts: "grace and peace." "Grace to you and peace from God our Father and the Lord Jesus Christ." The God who became human all the way—looking at us from the eyes of the Nazarene—speaks grace and peace to us—goes and dies for us, saying as he goes: " 'be of good cheer, I have overcome the world.' " (John 16:33)

"Grace . . . and peace from God our Father and the Lord Jesus Christ. . . . who will sustain you to the end." Who can believe that in our day, coming from one who seemed helpless to do anything but stretch out his hands for the nail? "Grace and peace" from *him?* Maybe we ought not to try and define it. Just reach out our hands and take it, from him "who will sustain you to the end." To the end of what? To the end of this hurting or death or both; this feeling of alienation, to the end of that shapeless, nameless darkness that lies somewhere at the center of your life; to the end of that—until the darkness yields to the light which God provides in his own way and in his own time.

There is someone for the hurting. I wonder what the old prophet would have said if he knew how God finally did it? At Bethlehem! Coming as flesh of our flesh. God for the hurting. God in the pain. God risen from the hurting and crowned with the pain!

This is where it all comes together—this believing in the

impossible. This is where we finally find the courage to live now, not giving up, learning to forgive and love, and to do our part to let this impossible love of God have its way in the world and in our own lives. It is in believing that the love of God has gotten into this world with both feet—in Jesus Christ. He is for the hurting. He is for you, just as you are, where you are. He is in the doubt and the fear. He is in the sin. He is in the hope and the joy of your living in the world he has made. He is ready to make you a friend to himself and neighbor to the world.

A Word After

This has been written in the hope that you will find some "green," where it seemed to be all brown around the edges. We began by asking, "Why live now?" We ended standing at a manger over which there is the shadow of a cross. Suppose God had asked that question—why live now—and had withdrawn? Suppose he is at the edge of your doubt, waiting quietly for you to believe his love? And suppose you do believe—what seems to be the impossible? I doubt that there will be any blinding light from above. Not an angel may stir a wing. After all, it is still "before breakfast." That "brown taste" may still be there. But as the day goes on, the faith held secret may bring its own quiet power. "Our faith," my friend George Buttrick once wrote me, "is a private piety and a public courage." I wish you good venture.

—Lee Stoffel

Notes

Chapter 1. It's Still Worth Living

1. From *The Poems of Gerard Manley Hopkins,* 4th ed. by W. H. Gardner and N. H. MacKenzie (London: Oxford University Press, 1967), no. 150, p. 186.

Chapter 2. Scraping the Bottom of the Barrel

1. John Buchan, *The Thirty-Nine Steps* (London: Thomas Nelson and Sons, Ltd., 1960), p. vi.

Chapter 5. Believing Someone Is for Us

1. As quoted in *Man, the Believer* by Samuel H. Miller (Nashville: Abingdon Press, 1968), p. 104.

Chapter 9. Finding the Freedom to Love

1. From *Sermons to Intellectuals,* ed. Franklin H. Littell (New York: Macmillan Publishing Co., 1963), pp. 85–86. © Franklin H. Littell 1963.

Chapter 12. Helping Others to Be Human

1. William Muehl, *All the Damned Angels* (Philadelphia: United Church Press, 1972), p. 26.

Chapter 16. Believing in Three Impossible Things before Breakfast

1. Lewis Carroll, *Through the Looking-Glass,* chapter 5.

Chapter 17. Not Giving Up

1. Joey Adams, *The God Bit* (New York: Mason/Charter Publishers, Inc., 1974), p. xiii.

2. *The Poems of Gerard Manley Hopkins,* no. 154, p. 193.

3. Loren Eiseley, *The Unexpected Universe* (New York: Harcourt, Brace & World, 1969), p. 71.

Chapter 18. The Years Are Not Empty

1. "Joy to the World!" from Psalm 98, Isaac Watts, 1719.